PRAYERS
TO
GO

© 2020 by Bisi and Toyin Tofade
All rights reserved.

No part of this book may be reproduced in any form or by any means, electronic or mechanical, including photocopying, recording, video, or by any information or retrieval system, without prior written permission from the publisher except for the use of brief quotations in a book review.

All Bible reference hyperlinks are to the King James Version.

Published in the United States by Uriel Press, a division of UMI
P.O. Box 436987, Chicago, IL 60643
www.urielpress.com

ISBN: 978-0-9601047-0-3 (paperback)
ISBN: 978-0-9601047-1-0 (eBook)

Cover and Book Design: Astrid Lewis Reedy

For more information about speaking engagements with Pastors Bisi and Toyin Tofade or to order multiple copies of this title, please email: pastorbisi@jubileenc.org

Printed in the United States of America

PRAYERS
TO
GO

Simple & Powerful Prayers for Challenging Times

BISI & TOYIN TOFADE

Introduction

100 Topical Life Situations
Over 1,000 Simple, Powerful Prayers
to Deal With Them

Many people want, and actually love, to pray. The problem is they do not know what to pray. Troubles and challenges of life are real and often overwhelming. One way to overcome them is through prayer.

In this book is a list of common challenges we all face at one time or another, and powerful prayer points for such times. You do not need to be a prayer expert to pray these prayers; they are for everyday use. Also included are scriptural verses you can refer to as you pray over each topic. Consider this a "Pocket Prayer Book."

Give this prayer book to your children to help them pray when they are in trouble. Give it to your friends, your spouse, your parents, and grandparents, and they will be on their way knowing what to pray when the occasion demands.

Blessings,

Dr. Alfred Bisi Tofade

Prayer Made Easy: Learning to Pray

Praying to God is a breath away. The same way we speak to a friend, child, or parent and they hear us without nerve-racking effort is the same way we commune with God. God is even closer! He can read our thoughts, hear our silent whispers and even our faintest cry.

The Power of Prayer

Prayer closed the mouth of lions. It was prayer that brought down walls. Prayer stopped the movement of the sun and the moon and brought down fire from heaven. It sealed the heaven for three and a half years and brought down rain again in the days of Elijah.

Prayer opened the prison doors and Peter walked away a free man. Whatever prayer cannot do is what God cannot—and there is nothing.

Jacob prayed until his name was changed, Jabez prayed until the curse was broken, and Hezekiah prayed until his life span was extended by 15 years. God delights in the prayer of ordinary people like you and me.

Praying for yourself is called petition, while praying for others is called intercession. Prayer can cross any barrier, cut across the oceans and continents, and travel faster than the speed of light. Prayer affects the present and controls the future. Prayer is invisible yet potent. Take prayer seriously.

How Do We Pray?

- Approach God reverently as a Father.
- Release your faith, believe He hears you and delights to answer you.
- Use His Word as much as you can. His promises are like precedence in a law court; He honors them.
- Confess your sins to Him, especially if you have things bothering your mind.
- Speak to Him in your own simple way without pretense or trying to impress Him. He understands every language on earth, even the street slangs.
- Include thanksgiving in your prayer. Cultivate the habit of entering His presence with a song of praise or simply thank Him for who He is to you and what He does.
- Finally, if you are filled with the Holy Spirit, allow Him to help you in your prayer life.

PRAYER PROVERBS

"Keep a secret and it is yours;
tell it to God and it's prayer;
tell it to people and it's gossip."

"Prayer is measured by its depth,
not necessarily its length."

"Satan: Blessed is he who
has no time to pray,
for he will become an easy prey."

"The tragedy of our day is not unanswered
prayer but unoffered prayer."

"The tallest man on earth is
the one on his knees."

"Life is fragile—handle with prayer."

How To Use This Book

This book divides various life challenges into 100 categories. You can easily find what applies to you from the Table of Contents.

The prayers in each category can be covered one at a time, depending on how much time you have. The prayer points can also be prayed as a single item under each category as needed.

The prayers can be read as declarations, confessions, or petitions. You can also expand on each point as the Holy Spirit inspires. Also note if you purchased the eBook, the key scripture references are linked to an online Bible so you can access the Word with ease. All references are to the King James Version.

Happy Praying!

COMING SOON

Look for our prayer app
(iOS & Android)
to use with this prayer book at
www.delightfulbooks.net.

TABLE OF CONTENTS

Introduction   5

Prayer Made Easy: Learning to Pray   6

How To Use This Book   9

1. When You Are Afraid 17
2. When in Debt 18
3. When Marriage Is Falling Apart 19
4. When Your Children Are in Trouble 20
5. When You Are Facing Trouble at Work 21
6. When You Are Rejected and Hated 22
7. When You Are Sick and Need Healing 23
8. When You Are Depressed and Sad 24
9. When You Are About to Choose a Marriage Partner 25
10. When You Are Confused 26
11. When You Are Disappointed 27
12. When You Are Financially Down and Broke 28
13. When You Are Getting Married 29
14. When You Have a Difficult Boss 30
15. When You Are Retiring 31
16. When You Need Progress and Acceleration in Life ... 32
17. When You Are Facing Family Crisis 33

18.	When You Are Facing Storms of Life	34
19.	When You Are Jobless	35
20.	When You Are Lonely	36
21.	When You Have a Court Case	37
22.	When You Are Writing Examinations	38
23.	When Your Business Is in Trouble or Fails	39
24.	When You Are Dealing With Anger	40
25.	When You Are Facing Disaster	41
26.	When You Need to Pray for Your Government	42
27.	When You Are Divorced or Going Through Divorce	43
28.	When There Is Death in the Family or Bereavement	44
29.	When Your Heart Is Broken	45
30.	When You Are Traveling or on a Journey	46
31.	When You Are Under Demonic Attack	47
32.	When You Are Troubled	48
33.	For Male Children	49
34.	For Female Children	50
35.	For Your Teenagers	51
36.	For Your Grandchildren	52
37.	For Your Grandparents	53
38.	For Your Extended Family	54

39.	When You Are Barren	55
40.	When You Lose Valuables	56
41.	When You Need Protection	57
42.	When You Need Favor	58
43.	When You Need a Wife	59
44.	When You Need a Husband	60
45.	When You Are Starting a New Business	61
46.	When You Are Persecuted	62
47.	When You Fail	63
48.	Prayer for Your Husband	64
49.	Prayer for Your Wife	65
50.	Overcoming Tragedies	66
51.	When Facing Temptations	67
52.	When You Are Seeking to Know the Will of God	68
53.	When You Are Struggling With Bad Habits and Addiction	69
54.	When You Are Making a Career Change	70
55.	When You Are Tired and Exhausted and Stressed Out	71
56.	When You Need to Forgive	72
57.	When You Are Seeking Wisdom	73
58.	When You Are Seeking Guidance and Direction	74
59.	Prayer for Your Parents	75

60. Prayer for Your Friends 76
61. When You Feel Discouraged and Want to Give Up 77
62. When You Are Facing Danger 78
63. When You Are in Spiritual Bondage 79
64. When You Are Perplexed and Overwhelmed 80
65. When Marking Your Birthday 81
66. When Your Faith Is Weak 82
67. When Facing Discrimination 83
68. When Your Relationship Fails and Falls Apart 84
69. When You Need Peace 85
70. When You Need Salvation 86
71. When You Just Had a Baby 87
72. Prayer for Infants and Newborns 88
73. When You Need Comfort 89
74. When in Courtship 90
75. When Starting a New Job 91
76. When There Is a National Disaster 92
77. When Relocating or Moving to a New House 93
78. When Dealing with Disability 94
79. When You Are in an Accident 95
80. When You Make a Costly Mistake 96
81. When You Need a Miracle or a Breakthrough 97

82. When You Just Graduate or for Your Graduate Children or Friends 98
83. When You Are Pregnant 99
84. When You Need Victory in Battles 100
85. When You Need Confidence 101
86. When Entering a New Year 102
87. When You Are in Conflict 103
88. When You Are Facing Delays 104
89. When You Have Bad Dreams or Nightmares 105
90. When You Are Stagnated and Need Promotion 106
91. When You Are in the Middle of a Crisis 107
92. Prayer for Your Pastor 108
93. Prayer for Troubled and Difficult Children 109
94. When You Cannot Sleep 110
95. When You Are Anxious or Worried 111
96. When You Mess Up and Seek Forgiveness 112
97. When You Are Facing Shame, Ridicule, and Embarrassment 113
98. When You Need Divine Intervention 114
99. When You Are at a Dead End of Life 115
100. When You Need Help, Support, and Favor From People 116

Steps Towards Salvation   **117**

About the Authors   **118**

1. When You Are Afraid

F-E-A-R: False Evidence Appearing Real
Isaiah 41:10, 2 Timothy 1:7, Psalm 27:1

- Father, I reject right now the spirit of fear in my life.
- I receive and operate in the spirit of power, love, and sound mind.
- I rebuke every evil spirit bringing fear into my life.
- Lord, grant me serenity and peace in my heart. Help me to trust you at this moment of fear and panic.
- Father, I pray that you turn what I am afraid of into blessing and testimony.
- I shall not be afraid of evil tidings, my heart is fixed, trusting the Lord.
- The Lord is my light and my salvation; whom shall I fear? The Lord is the strength of my life; of whom shall I be afraid?
- I release right now what I am afraid of into the hands of the Lord: my past, my future, the fear of man, the fear of the known and unknown.
- Lord, remove everything that has troubled my heart, take out whatever is trying to steal my peace and confidence.
- In righteousness, I shall be established: I shall be far from oppression; for I shalt not fear: and from terror; for it shall not come near me.

2. When in Debt

Philippians 4:19, Deuteronomy 15:6, Proverbs 22:7

- Lord, make a way for me out of debt and free me from the burden of debt.

- Open my eyes to see what to do to free myself from debt. Show me the way out of this and reveal solutions to me.

- I ask you to grant me financial discipline and wisdom to manage my resources.

- Remove from my life every greed, covetousness, and mistake that brought me into debt.

- Father, deliver me from the trap of debt, set my shoulders free from its burden.

- In Jesus' Name, I ask for financial miracle and breakthrough to break the cycle of debt over my life.

- I loosen myself from the bondage of financial setback, financial struggle, and the spirit of lack.

- I receive financial empowerment to lend to nations and not to be a borrower.

- In Jesus' Name, I receive the miracle of debt cancellation. Let your power bring down the mountain of debt in my life.

- I come against unforeseen problems and challenges that drain my finances. I rebuke demonic devourers out of my life.

3. When Marriage Is Falling Apart
Matthew 19:6, Genesis 2:24, Ecclesiastes 4:9

- Father, heal my marriage by your divine power.
- I ask that you divinely intervene on behalf of me and my spouse and release the miracle of restoration.
- Holy Spirit, reveal the solution to our marital problems and give us understanding on what to do.
- I decree and declare that the forces of evil attacking my marriage be overthrown.
- Lord, grant us the ability to forgive one another. I seek your wisdom to resolve our differences peacefully.
- In Jesus' Name, I completely uproot bitterness, animosity, hatred, misunderstanding, and any other evil seed the enemy has sown into my marriage.
- Lord, bring oneness and unity into my marriage that we will cleave together again.
- The Lord shall heal and restore my home.
- I pray for a fresh release of love and affection into my marriage. Lord put fresh wine of love into our union.
- My marriage will not fail, my marriage will not collapse.
- I take a stand against all external forces and influences working against my marriage to destabilize it.
- I reject the spirit of strife hovering over my marriage. I command the plans of the enemy to fail.

4. When Your Children Are in Trouble

Isaiah 49:24-25, Psalm 127:3, James 1:5

- Oh Lord, stretch out your mighty hands and rescue my child(ren) from trouble and imminent dangers.
- I thank you and I declare that the children you have given me are for signs and wonders.
- I pray over_____ that the spirit of rebellion will be removed from his/her life.
- I ask that you fill my child(ren) with the needed wisdom to deliver him/her from this current situation.
- I pray to remove ungodly influences around his life and shield him from wrong counsel.
- I ask, Lord, that you will choose the right friends for my children.
- I pray to overthrow the forces of evil that want to derail the destinies of my children.
- Lord, send helpers of destiny to my children and help them out of the current problems.
- I speak the peace of the Lord over my children right now.
- Lord, I ask that you help my children overcome temptations and every trap the enemy set for them.
- I pray for angelic intervention at every turn of their lives.
- I pray that you will cover my children with a shield of favor and mercy.

5. When You Are Facing Trouble at Work
Psalm 34:4-6, Psalm 90:17, Daniel 6:1-4

- In Jesus' Name, I command "peace be still" to every wind of problem blowing in my workplace.
- Father, turn the hearts of my bosses to favor me.
- Lord, remove every hatred and discrimination around my person.
- I receive wisdom to sort out every trouble and challenge at work.
- Father, I declare that the atmosphere in my workplace shall become conducive to work.
- Lord, shut the mouth of all my accusers and frustrate the counsel of my adversaries.
- I pray that you grant me the grace to be patient, loving, and tolerant of my coworkers.
- I declare and decree that I will not lose my job. I will not be displaced or replaced.
- Help me by your spirit to do my work diligently and excellently as expected of me. I will not be slothful, careless, or complacent.

6. When You Are Rejected and Hated

Psalm 18:16-19, Psalm 27:10, Isaiah 41:10

- Lord, I pray that you remove from my life the spirit of disfavor.
- Lord, I ask that you cover me with the shield of favor.
- Lord, I pray that you disappoint the expectations of those looking to find faults with me.
- Lord, arise in battle and fight for me. Speak for me where I have no voice.
- I pray Lord that you will turn this hatred to my advantage.
- Touch the hearts of those who hate me for no cause. Put my love in their hearts.
- I rebuke the evil spirit behind this hatred. I discomfit the power of darkness engineering the hate against me.
- Lord, help me to love and not to hate. I will not retaliate or seek vengeance against my adversary. Help me to forgive them.

7. When You Are Sick and Need Healing

Isaiah 53:3-5, Exodus 15:26, Jeremiah 30:17

- Lord, I ask by faith for your healing power to flow into my life.
- I receive my healing right now from____ (mention the sickness).
- In the name of Jesus, I rebuke the affliction of____ (mention the sickness).
- I confess that by the stripes that Jesus took for me, I am made whole.
- Remove every trace of this sickness from my body and flush it out from my bloodstream.
- Revive every organ in my body, renew every tissue, restore my health to a perfect state.
- I confess my sins, unforgiveness, and bitterness in my life that may block the flow of your healing power.
- I confess you as my Great Physician, touch every part of my body, soul, and spirit and make me whole.
- I confess that I will live and not die to declare the goodness of the Lord in the land of the living.
- I decree and declare my deliverance and healing according to God's word and I pray for its manifestation right now.

8. When You Are Depressed and Sad

Psalm 42:11, Psalm 30:11-12, John 16:33

- ❧ I ask in prayer that the joy of the Lord will flow again into my life.
- ❧ Father, I ask for forgiveness of any known or unknown sin in my life that could have opened the doors to afflictions.
- ❧ I exchange the garment of heaviness for the spirit of praise.
- ❧ I pray that you will heal my heart, my mind, and my soul.
- ❧ Lord, send glad tidings and good news to my life. Let my bones be revived.
- ❧ I command sadness and depression to loosen their hold from my life right now in Jesus' Name.
- ❧ I confess and declare that the joy of the Lord is my strength. Holy Spirit, lift me up in my soul and fill me with gladness.
- ❧ Dear Lord, help me to focus on you and the things you have done for me and to take my eyes from the negative things around me.
- ❧ I displace every weight that is weighing down my soul, and I cast out every spirit of anxiety and worry.

9. When You Are About to Choose a Marriage Partner

Proverbs 18:22, Psalm 37:4, Ecclesiastes 4:9-11

- Lord, grant me divine guidance and direction as I make this important decision of my life.
- I pray that you open my eyes of understanding and grant me divine revelation.
- Lord, help me that I will not choose wrongly or be led by sight.
- I release my help-meet and receive him/her by faith.
- In the Name of Jesus, I reject confusion and misdirection in my life. Lord, let me not go astray.
- Lord, I pray that you confirm your will in my life by revealing to me the bones of my bones. Confirm with an evident sign.
- Lord, I pray against unnecessary delay in life. Your plans for me will not be placed on hold.
- Father speak clearly to my spirit, remove every ambiguity that can lead to confusion.
- I give you thanks because your plans for me are good and you will give me a beautiful future.
- I refuse to fret or panic as I make this choice. I reject fear and every form of anxiety.

10. When You Are Confused

John 14:26, Proverbs 3:5, 2 Corinthians 10:5

- Father, I desire that you give me clarity.
- Let your light penetrate through every darkness in my mind and illuminate my understanding.
- I confess you have not given me confusion but a sound mind.
- Holy Spirit, shed your light abroad in my heart, speak quietly to my soul, and reveal the will of the Father to me.
- Show me which way I should go and lead me in the path of life. Where there is darkness, shed your light.
- I use my authority in the Name of Jesus to bind and cast out the spirit of confusion, doubt, and unbelief from my life.
- Dear Lord, release good counsel to me and use good people to give me direction out of the current situation.
- Lord, I rest my faith in you. I shall not go astray or make a wrong turn in life. Grant me peace and joy in all my choices.
- Lord, make your face to shine upon me and let your strong Hands keep my feet from slipping into danger.

11. When You Are Disappointed

Philippians 4:6-7, Romans 8:28, Psalm 121:1-2

- Lord, help me to handle the disappointment I am currently facing with a positive spirit.
- I refuse in the name of the Lord to sink into the pit of disappointment.
- I forgive everyone responsible for this disappointment. I refuse to hold grudges and bitterness against them.
- Father, help me to turn this disappointment around and bring something good out of it.
- Father, forgive me in every way I am responsible for this disappointing situation.
- Help me to put my trust in you and not in man or their promises.
- Lord, show me the way out of this current situation and lead me to victory.
- Father, let me not be ashamed because I put my trust in you. Though men may disappoint me, you can never disappoint.

12. When You Are Financially Down and Broke

Philippians 4:19, Psalm 37:25-26, Isaiah 33:16

- Lord, turn my financial table around and let the season of dryness end in my life.
- I declare you are my Jehovah Jireh, you will supply my needs according to your riches in glory.
- I come against every form of devourer in my life. I close the door to financial leakage in my life.
- Father, I pray you will touch the hearts of people on my behalf to bless me.
- In the Name of Jesus, Lord, open my eyes to my opportunities around the world.
- I reject and rebuke the spirit of lack and poverty in my life and family.
- I declare and decree a season of abundance and plenty in my life.
- Lord, help me to be faithful and obedient to you in my financial life.
- Lord, I pray you will grant me wisdom for financial breakthrough.
- Father, I ask that you bless the works of my hands and increase me on every side.
- Lord, help me to have a heart of giving and a life free from covetousness.

13. When You Are Getting Married

2 Timothy 1:12, Matthew 19:6, Ephesians 5:28,33

- Thank you, Lord, for providing a good spouse for my future.
- Father, I ask that you prepare me and my future mate for a future of marital happiness.
- Grant to me and my mate your peace and blessings to enjoy our future married life.
- Jesus, I ask that you provide for all our needs according to your riches in glory.
- I pray that every evil plan of the enemy against our day of celebration will be aborted.
- Lord, I ask for safety on the road, air, sea, or rail for everyone planning to attend our wedding.
- I decree and declare that there shall be no confusion, commotion, or contention on our wedding day.
- I cover all the wedding party, officials, and attendees with the blood of Jesus. I pray all shall go well.
- Lord, I ask that you will join us together. You will knit our hearts together and make us one.
- In Jesus' Name, I pray that our two families will be in unity and one accord as we prepare for our wedding. I remove disunity, disagreement, selfishness, and division.
- I pray that the Lord will be glorified on our wedding day and in our marriage.

14. When You Have a Difficult Boss

2 Timothy 1:7, Proverbs 16:7, Psalm 23:4

- Lord, touch the heart of my boss to favor me.
- Remove hatred and animosity towards me from his/her heart.
- Father, grant me wisdom to behave wisely with him/her.
- Put my affection and love in his/her heart.
- Lord, let my work environment be positive and friendly. Remove every tension and negative spirit at my workplace.
- Let peace and mutual understanding reign and rule at my workplace.
- I reject every spirit behind gossips, slander, and character assassination from my place of work.
- I eliminate the spirit of suspicion and envy from my work environment.
- Let my work be satisfying and help me do my job with an excellent spirit.
- Lord, replace conflict with love, hatred and animosity with affection and a caring spirit.

15. When You Are Retiring

Psalm 92:12-14, Psalm 71:9, Hebrews 6:10

- Lord, I give thanks for all the years of service, for grace and strength.
- Lord, I pray that you prepare me for my retirement years (physically, spiritually, financially, etc.).
- Lord, I commit my retired years to your hands. Grant me peace and joy.
- Father, I pray that my latter years shall be the best of my years on earth.
- I ask that you grant me good health and strength, that I will not be sickly and weak.
- Lord, continue to use me as a blessing to my children and grandchildren and to the world at large.
- I pray that I shall not be miserable in my latter years. Lord, take care of me physically, emotionally, financially, and spiritually.
- Grant me joy and fulfillment in my life. Remove sorrow and regrets far from me.
- I pray that I will live long and fulfill my days on earth. My life will not be cut short.
- I declare that I will be fruitful and flourishing even in my retirement years.
- I confess and declare that strange diseases, cancer, terminal ailments, etc. shall not invade my body.
- I shall not be disabled or become a liability in my old age.

16. When You Need Progress and Acceleration in Life

Proverbs 4:18, 1 Kings 18:46, Psalm 37:37

- Lord, I give you thanks for every good thing you have done in my life up to this moment.
- I desire that there shall be increase in my life in every facet.
- I decree and declare against the forces of stagnation and lack of progress.
- Father, I pray that you will open new doors of opportunities for me in life.
- In the Name of Jesus, let my path shine brighter and brighter each day.
- I desire and pray that I will grow and prosper in my career, my family life, and my spiritual life.
- Father, I pray that you will divinely and forcefully move me forward in life. I shall not be behind; I shall be the head and not the tail.
- Lord, I ask for divine enablement to overtake and outrun those who have gone ahead of me.
- I break the hold of limitations and containment in my life. Let the ceilings of limitations be shattered.
- I prophesy a complete turnaround in my life. Let promotion come over my life.
- I declare divine acceleration today; my path shall open up and my steps shall be accelerated.

17. When You Are Facing Family Crisis

Psalm 34:6, Psalm 50:15, Deuteronomy 31:6

- Lord, deliver me and my family from every evil plan of the enemy.
- I ask for wisdom and understanding from the Lord to resolve the current crisis rocking my family.
- Father, I ask for divine intervention in this family crisis, and I receive divine solutions to these problems.
- Lord, I receive your mercy and compassion on behalf of my family.
- I ask in the Name of Jesus for your hands of miracles to bring about the needed blessings for my family at this point in time.
- Lord, open our eyes of understanding to see the door of deliverance you have made available for us to escape this crisis.
- Father, I ask that you send your angels to us in the form of helpers and resources that are needed to resolve this crisis.
- I close the door against the enemy and forces of darkness that are trying to destabilize our family.
- I declare and decree restoration of peace and all that the devil stole from our family.

18. When You Are Facing Storms of Life

Mark 4:35-41, Nahum 1:7, Psalm 91:1-2

- In the Name of Jesus, I arrest this evil wind blowing against my life.
- I decree that the storm around my life be still and calm.
- Jesus, hold my hands through this ravaging storm, let me not drown in it.
- Father, strengthen my faith through the storm of life, let my faith not fail.
- According to your word, Lord, surround me with your presence, I will not be afraid.
- Turn around every storm blowing in my life, job, career, family, and marriage to a blessing in disguise.
- I refuse to sink in this storm. I shall not die but live to declare the good works of the Lord.
- Lord, give me the strength to overcome this storm and every attack of the enemy against my life.
- Father, be my refuge, my rock, and my fortress and hide me in your pavilion until this storm pass.
- I confess my victory and dominion in the middle of this turmoil. I declare I am more than a conqueror over it.

19. When You Are Jobless

Matthew 6:33, 2 Thessalonians 3:10

- Thank you, Lord, for giving me strength and good health to work.

- I pray that job opportunities begin to open for me in different sectors of the economy.

- Father, I pray that your spirit will direct and order my steps to the right job.

- Lord, grant me supernatural favor with people that I will meet at my job interviews.

- I pray that you will quicken my name in the hearts of the people that will interview me, and I will be favored in their sight.

- I come against lack and frustration in my job search. Grant me heavenly assistance with this effort.

- In the Name of the Lord, I refuse to give up, I refuse to be discouraged.

- I ask that you grant me the grace to prepare my resume properly and to be ready for my interviews. I shall not be careless.

- I receive now my miracle job. I give you thanks for it in advance.

- Lord, make way for me in the wilderness, make room for me in this land, provide for me in this wilderness.

20. When You Are Lonely
Isaiah 41:10, Psalm 25:16, Hebrews 13:5

- Lord, I thank you that you are with me. I thank you for the gift of life.
- Lord, fill my heart with joy and gratefulness.
- Lord, I pray you will send great friends to my life.
- I ask that the awareness of your presence dawn on me, and I will not be afraid or feel lonely.
- Father, I pray that you will reveal to me whatever may be missing in my life. Grant me the grace to overcome them.
- Open my eyes to opportunities to do good things around me and in the community.
- I rebuke and resist the spirit of depression and sadness in my life. The joy of the Lord is my strength.
- Father, cause me to find comfort in your word and encourage me by your presence.
- Father, I receive the companionship of the Holy Spirit now. Fill me with your peace.
- Lord, release good company into my life, friends and companions that will cheer me up.

21. When You Have a Court Case

Psalm 121:1, Psalm 46:1, 2 Chronicles 20:17

- In the Name of Jesus, I ask that your presence will remove from my life every spirit of fear.
- Lord, grant me boldness and confidence and to the attorney representing me in this case.
- I pray that you will protect me from false allegations and false witnesses.
- Father, let the truth prevail. Let lies and falsehoods fall flat.
- Jesus, I pray that you will grant me divine favor before the judge and the jury.
- Jesus, I declare you are my advocate, you are my attorney. Arise and stand up for my defense.
- I cover my heart with the blood of Jesus; deliver me from the spirit of hate, revenge, and grudges.
- In Jesus' Name, no weapon of the enemy fashioned against me shall prevail. You will shut up the mouth of my false accusers.
- Father, fill my heart with your peace. I shall not be anxious or panic.
- Above all, I pray that God will be glorified in this case. You will vindicate me and protect your good name in my life.

22. When You Are Writing Examinations

Daniel 1:20, Deuteronomy 28:13, Isaiah 50:7

- Lord Jesus, prepare me physically and emotionally for this examination.
- I rebuke the spirit of fear. I shall not be anxious and overwhelmed.
- I come to you in faith to ask for wisdom, even as you gave Daniel, to pass my exams with flying colors.
- Father, I receive divine guidance to read relevant materials for this exam. Show me what to do.
- Lord, grant me retentive memory to remember all that I have read and will be reading. Strengthen my memory power.
- Holy Spirit, remind me of all that I have read; give me the insight to answer all the questions correctly.
- Lord, let your presence be with me throughout this examination. Send your angels to surround me and minister to me.
- I declare success, I shall not be the tail, but I shall be the head. I shall not be beneath but above.
- Lord, let me find your favor with my examiners. Let nothing count against me.
- I proclaim victory now; I receive divine help now. I shall testify to your goodness and help.

23. When Your Business Is in Trouble or Fails

Isaiah 48:17, Deuteronomy 28:13, Psalm 1:3

- Heavenly Father, I ask that you turn my business around.
- I thank you for your promises of success and prosperity.
- I stand in the Name of the Lord against every devourer and attack ravaging my business.
- Lord, help me to recover everything I have lost in business. I receive now the grace of recovery and restoration.
- Jesus, help me to make the right decision that will affect my business positively.
- Father, grant me the wisdom needed for business success to turn my business around.
- Lord, I commit my work and business into your hands. Let my plans succeed.
- Lord, give me the right partners that will help me to take my business to the next level.
- I receive in the Name of Jesus, the financial breakthrough needed for my business to succeed.
- Father, help me to overcome and settle all debts and any other factors that have crippled my business.

24. When You Are Dealing With Anger

Proverbs 16:32, James 1:19-20, Ephesians 4:31

- Lord, help me to defeat the spirit of anger in my life.
- Help me, Father, to identify the issues causing provocation and anger in my life.
- Lord, give me peace of mind and calmness in my soul.
- Father, forgive me and cleanse me from anger, animosity, and hatred.
- In Jesus' Name, I come against the spirit of pride and arrogance in my life behind my anger.
- I reject the spirit of strife in my life and against my life. Help me to overcome hatred, bitterness, and animosity in my life.
- Fill my life with kindness, patience, love, long-suffering, and tolerance for other people.
- I come against the atmosphere of hostility around my workplace, my family, and all my relationships.
- Lord, I release all my accusers and everyone who has offended me in the past and currently.
- Holy Spirit, I ask that you breathe on me and work in me to overcome the spirit of anger.

25. When You Are Facing Disaster
Psalm 9:9, Psalm 46:1

- Lord, I confess you are my deliverer, my helper, and my restorer.
- Dear Jesus, still the storm, avert the disaster for me.
- Lord, I frustrate and overthrow all spiritual hurricane facing my family, marriage, and finances.
- I put my confidence in you, Lord, and confess you as the rock of refuge and anchor to my soul.
- Father, arise to my defense, fight on my behalf, and win the victory for me.
- Jesus, let the enemy behind this situation be defeated and put to shame.
- Because I trust in you, I shall not be confounded or ashamed in life.
- Father, I receive the spirit of peace, and I release myself from fear and anxiety.
- I bind the violent spirit behind this raging storm, and I declare, "Peace be still."
- Thank you, Lord because you are the Master over the storm of life. You are with me in this boat right now and I believe my boat shall not sink.

26. When You Need to Pray for Your Government

1 Timothy 2:1-3, Proverbs 11:14, Jeremiah 29:7

- I speak peace over my nation, I decree and declare the presence of the Lord.
- I destroy and dismantle the power of the enemy influencing this nation.
- Let the fear of the Lord rule the hearts of everyone in the place of authority.
- Father, I pray for the president, that you will grant him boldness to stand up for righteousness and rule in the fear of God.
- I uproot ungodliness and unrighteousness running rampant over this land.
- I pray for stability in our government, society, and families.
- I pray for your protection over the lives of all our legislators, judges, governors, and mayors.
- I decree that righteousness shall fill our streets, our young people shall be preserved, and peace will fill our lives.
- Lord, cause our rulers to know what is right and grant them wisdom to rule without discrimination.
- Remove corruption, bribery, evil, and all manner of ungodliness from our leadership and the people that rule our land.

27. When You Are Divorced or Going Through Divorce

Hebrews 13:5, Isaiah 49:15-16

- ⤞ Lord, I give you thanks for being my support and help in this difficult situation and season of my life.
- ⤞ Father, I pray that you will bring your healing to my heart and everyone that is hurting because of this situation.
- ⤞ I pray that you will grant me and my ex the spirit of forgiveness and reconciliation so that our healing process can begin.
- ⤞ Dear Lord, I ask that you restore all that the enemy has stolen from my life, physically, emotionally, and spiritually.
- ⤞ Let your peace return into my life and the lives of my children and my extended family.
- ⤞ Father, let your presence surround me and the children at this difficult time and make it vivid to us.
- ⤞ Grant me wisdom and understanding on how to move on from this moment forward.
- ⤞ I pray that all outstanding court cases be discharged peacefully and all matters resolved amicably.
- ⤞ Lord, work in the hearts of our children to go through this difficult situation peacefully and grant them strength and grace to prevail.
- ⤞ Lord, grant me the joy of your abiding presence and meet all my needs.

28. When There Is Death in the Family or Bereavement

2 Corinthians 1:3-4, Psalm 147:3, Psalm 73:26

- ⊹ Lord, I thank you because you are in control right now.
- ⊹ Father, we trust you completely that you know the best in every situation, and you are a wise God even when we don't understand a thing.
- ⊹ I speak your peace and comfort to every heart that is broken and bruised.
- ⊹ Holy Spirit, I pray that you will release your power and anointing to bring the needed word of consolation and comfort to our hearts.
- ⊹ Father, I pray that you will grant us the strength and serenity to bear this loss and fill our hearts with a sense of your nearness.
- ⊹ Jesus, replace the pain in our hearts with your peace, the sorrow with joy.
- ⊹ Lord, I pray that you will fill the vacuum our beloved _____ left in our family and our hearts.
- ⊹ Lord, give us the knowledge and faith to walk with at this moment of grief and difficulty.
- ⊹ Manifest your love in our lives in unusual ways at this moment. Help our family to stay strong and united in your love. I speak long life over my family. We will fulfill our days.
- ⊹ In Jesus' Name, I bind every spirit of heaviness and depression over the family. I bind the spirit of premature death over our family.

29. When Your Heart Is Broken

Isaiah 40:1, 2 Thessalonians 2:16-17

- Lord, I thank you because you are my strength and joy.
- Lord, I pray that you will heal my heart and bring restoration and peace.
- Jesus, put my heart together again. Flush out pain, disappointment, and bitterness.
- Make my heart whole again. Lord, help my heart to lean and trust in you.
- Father, I pray that you will change every disappointment of my life to divine appointment.
- I release everyone that has hurt me voluntarily, and I forgive every offense against me.
- Jesus, I pour my heart to you, lift up the heaviness and the burden that is my heart.
- Breathe freshness into my spirit, let my heart rejoice in your presence.
- Savior, I release into your hands right now everything that has broken my heart. I refuse to carry this burden by myself.
- Lord, wipe away my sorrow, remove the tears in my eyes. Put joy in my heart and laughter on my lips.

30. When You Are Traveling or on a Journey
Psalm 121:7-8, Psalm 91:4

- Father, I thank you for your continual protection over my life always.
- In Jesus' Name, I cover this trip with the blood of Jesus.
- I speak safety to the airways, road, sea, and railways. I declare safety on the wheels and in the air or the sea.
- I frustrate the plans of the enemy to bring accidents, disaster, or danger on this trip.
- Lord, let your hands be upon the driver, pilots, captain, or anyone associated with the coordination of this trip.
- Lord, keep us healthy and safe from illness, health breakdown, or any hazard that may come with this trip.
- I bind every blood-sucking demon on the air, road, or seaways.
- I cover all properties, loved ones, and family with the blood of Jesus. We will return to meet everything in safety.
- I decree and declare that we will not experience violence, robbery, or any form of attack on this trip.
- Thank you, Jesus, for journey mercies.

31. When You Are Under Demonic Attack
Isaiah 54:17, Jeremiah 1:19

- Heavenly Father, thank you because I am washed and covered by the blood of Jesus.
- I declare now in the name of Jesus that no weapon fashioned against me shall prosper.
- I am covered and marked by the blood over my life. Demons, I command you to remove your hands from my life.
- Lord, I shut every door through which the enemy is attacking me right now. I close every open door in my life.
- Father, I confess every sin in my life. I renounce every act of disobedience and rebellion in my life.
- Lord, arise and fight for me. Take over every battle of my life.
- I reject now the spirit of fear. I will not be afraid because the Lord is my defense.
- In Jesus' Name, I speak the fire of the Holy Spirit around me right now. I command the fire of the Spirit to devour every wickedness and attack around my life.
- I decree and declare that this oppression will stop right now and the attacks will cease.
- I speak the word of victory, "touch not my anointed and do my servants no harm."

32. When You Are Troubled
Psalm 23:4, Psalm 27:5

- Lord, I give you thanks because you are my comforter and helper in the time of need.
- Father, I ask that your peace will fill my heart right now.
- Lord, grant me direction and instruction to know what to do in every situation of life.
- I destroy every spirit of confusion in my life. I overthrow every form of anxiety, anger, and restlessness in my life.
- I speak to every storm around my life to be at peace. I rebuke every wind of adversity and trouble to remove its hands from my life.
- Father, let your light shine on my path; help me to find direction and instruction for my life from your word.
- In time of trouble, hide me under your pavilion according to your word.
- Lord, I ask that you provide me the right solution to overcome every challenge and trouble confronting me right now.
- I give you thanks because you will grant me stability in the time of trouble, and I shall find your comfort.
- I pray that you will turn my situation around and bring glory to your name out of my trouble.

33. For Male Children

Psalm 144:11-13, Isaiah 44:3-4

- Lord, thank you for the gift of son(s).
- Lord, I pray that my sons shall be men of God and serve you like Samuel.
- Father, I declare that my sons shall be free from immorality, sexual sins, and any other form of uncleanliness.
- I desire that you make their minds pure and free them from all forms of spiritual bondage.
- I pray that they will not be caught in any entanglement, wrong associations, or with toxic or dangerous substances.
- Father, I pray that you will help them choose their friends and associates wisely. Separate them from wrong company.
- I ask that you give them wives after your heart who will be a source of blessing to their lives.
- I declare that no demonic influence will come near them. No violence or attack over their lives will succeed.
- I pray that my sons will be emotionally strong, spiritually sound, intellectually sharp, and morally pure.
- I pray for their success and prosperity in life. They will be blessed with great jobs and excel in life.

34. For Female Children
Psalm 144:11-13, Proverbs 31:29

- Lord thank you for the gift of daughter(s).
- Lord I pray that my daughter(s) shall be women of God and serve the Lord like Deborah.
- Father, I declare that my daughter(s) shall be free from immorality, sexual sins, and any other form of uncleanliness.
- I desire that you make their minds pure and free them from all forms of spiritual bondage.
- I pray that they will not be caught in any entanglement, wrong associations, or with toxic or dangerous substances.
- Father, I pray that you will help them choose their friends and associates wisely. Separate them from wrong company.
- I ask that you give them husbands after your heart who will be a source of blessing to their lives.
- I declare that no demonic influence will come near them. No violence or attack over their lives will succeed.
- I pray that my daughter(s) will be emotionally strong, spiritually sound, intellectually sharp, and morally pure.
- I pray for their success and prosperity in life. They will be blessed with great jobs and excel in life.
- I declare they will not be molested or violated by anyone.

35. For Your Teenagers
Isaiah 49:25, 1 Corinthians 10:13

- Thank you, Lord, for giving my children the grace to mature into adulthood.
- I pray that my teenage children shall love God and be free from the evil of the society. They will not depart from the right way.
- Father, I remove every ungodly peer pressure from their lives and deliver them from temptations.
- Father, I declare that my teenage children shall be free from immorality, sexual sins, and any other form of uncleanliness.
- I desire that you make their minds pure and free them from all forms of spiritual bondage.
- I pray that they will not be caught in any entanglement, wrong associations, or with toxic or dangerous substances.
- Father, I pray that you will help them choose their friends and associates wisely. Separate them from wrong company.
- I ask that you give them husbands and wives after your heart who will be a source of blessing to their lives.
- I declare that no demonic influence will come near them. No violence or attack over their lives will succeed.
- I pray that my teenage children will be emotionally strong, spiritually sound, intellectually sharp, and morally pure.
- I pray for their success and prosperity in life. They will be blessed with great jobs and excel in life.

36. For Your Grandchildren
Proverbs 17:6, Psalm 37:25, Proverbs 13:22

- Lord, I thank you for your blessings in my life and for giving me the grace to be a grandparent.
- Lord, I ask that your peace and blessing be on my grandchild(ren).
- Father, I pray for their protection and safety in life, that no harm will come upon them.
- Jesus, I pray that my grandchildren will grow to love you and shall be godly men and women.
- Father, I remove every ungodly peer pressure from their lives.
- Father, I declare that my teenage children shall be free from immorality, sexual sins, and any other form of uncleanliness.
- I desire that you make their minds pure and free them from all forms of spiritual bondage.
- I pray that they will not be caught in any entanglement, wrong associations, or with toxic or dangerous substances.
- Father, I pray that you will help them choose their friends and associates wisely. Separate them from wrong company.
- I ask that you give them husbands and wives after your heart who will be a source of blessing to their lives.
- I declare that no demonic influence will come near them. No violence or attack over their lives will succeed.
- I pray for their success and prosperity in life. They will be blessed with great jobs and excel in life.

37. For Your Grandparents

Psalm 92:14, Isaiah 40:28-31

- Lord, I give you thanks for the lives of my grandparents.
- I ask for strength and health for my grandparents. I pray that they will be free from diseases and afflictions of the body.
- I pray for sound mind for my grandparents. I pray they will be at peace in every area of their lives.
- Father, I ask that you protect them from Lord all forms of danger and calamity. Keep them safe from accidents.
- I receive divine provisions for my grandparents in their old age. I pray they will not lack and live in poverty.
- I pray that my grandparents will live full and fulfilled lives.
- Lord, fill my grandparents with great joy over their children and grandchildren. Grant them long life to enjoy their grandchildren.
- Lord, I desire that my grandparents will live long enough to see their great-grandchildren and enjoy them in their lives.
- Thank you, Lord, for watching continually over them and keeping them in perfect peace.

38. For Your Extended Family

Isaiah 26:3, Acts 16:31

- Father, I give you thanks because you are our protector and provider.
- I cover every member of my extended family with the precious blood of Jesus. I decree no one shall die before their time.
- Lord, I pray that you will protect each member of my extended family from dangers and calamities.
- I ask for divine provision to meet all their needs and make supplies available at the point of their needs.
- Preserve the lives of the young people in my family. Give our elders long life and good health.
- Lord, fill my extended family far and near with your joy and grant them breakthroughs in all their endeavors.
- I speak peace, love, and unity to my extended family. I root out division and the spirit of strife and animosity.
- Lord, I release abundance and prosperity over my extended family. I come against poverty and backwardness in our family.
- Lord, send your help to my family and bring your salvation to everyone. Open their eyes to see the light of your salvation.
- Thank you, Lord, for the preservation, provision, and protection for my family. There shall be no shedding of tears in our family.

39. When You Are Barren

Psalm 113:9, Isaiah 54:1, Exodus 23:25-26

- Father, I believe your word that it is your will that I be fruitful. There will be joyful celebrations of newborns.
- I, therefore, declare against unfruitfulness and barrenness in my/our lives as a couple.
- Lord Jesus, I pray for your healing over our lives. Remove from us every trace of disease, infirmity, or any genetic abnormalities.
- I declare and decree a release and liberty from any ancestral heritage that may work against our fruitfulness in any way.
- Satan, in Jesus' Name, I command you to remove your hands from our lives. I destroy every form of affliction against our lives.
- I prophesy that we will have healthy babies that will be carried to term.
- I destroy every form of miscarriage and premature birth. I close every door through which the enemy may try to steal our blessings.
- Heavenly Father, I pray that you will fulfill and perfect our joy. Grant to us a performance of our expectations.
- I invite you Holy Spirit to guide and direct us in the process of planning and preparing for conception.
- I refuse to be anxious, troubled, or overwhelmed by this need. I relax and release everything into the hands of our Maker. You will make all things beautiful in Your time.

40. When You Lose Valuables

Joel 2:25, John 10:10

- Lord, I give thanks that I did not lose my life.
- I ask that in your mercy, you will release the grace of restoration into my life.
- Lord, grant me peace of mind free from worry and anxiety because of what I lost.
- I ask, Lord, that every loophole and open door through which the enemy steals from my life be closed.
- Grant me the grace to be vigilant and alert to prevent future loss in my life.
- I arrest in the Name of Jesus every thief and devourer in my life and family.
- Lord, restore unto me what the years of cankerworms, palmerworms, and locusts stole from my life.
- For everything I have lost in life, Heavenly Father, I pray that you will restore them in multiple fold.
- Lord, take back for me what the enemy took from my life. Whosoever is in possession of my good, I command them to release it now.
- Thank you, Lord, because all shall be well eventually, and I will give you the glory. You will turn this trouble to triumph in my life.

41. When You Need Protection
Psalm 91:1-14, Zechariah 2:8

- Thank you, Lord, for your continuous protection in my life.
- Let the Lord arise on my behalf and scatter all my enemies. Let the arrows of the wicked be returned to their senders.
- Arise, Lord, to my defense and protect me from all evil.
- Deliver me from the snare of the enemy, let me not fall into the trap of the wicked.
- Keep me as the apple of your eyes, Lord. Let no arrows of the enemy touch my life.
- Lord, order my feet aright and direct me away from calamity.
- Lord, be my refuge, my shield and buckler. Keep me from accident and disaster.
- Let me not be at the wrong place at the wrong time with the wrong people.
- Dispatch your angels to accompany me at work, at home, and in all of my travels.
- Protect me from afflictions, diseases, stray bullets, assaults, demonic attacks, and everything that can cause me bodily harm.
- I plead the blood of Jesus over my life, my property, my house, my vehicle, and all that is around me.
- I cover my entire household and my family members by this powerful blood of Jesus.

42. When You Need Favor
Psalm 5:12, Psalm 102:13

- Lord, I give you praise for your everlasting love and kindness towards me.
- Father, I ask that you cover me with your favor as a shield wherever I go.
- Lord, cause me to find favor in unusual places and with people I don't know.
- I desire your favor in my business, on my job, or at my workplace.
- Jesus, let me find favor with my boss, my spouse, my superiors, and among my friends.
- I declare that I have favor today to receive your blessings needed in my life.
- I declare that because of your favor over my life, I shall not struggle or lack. One day of your favor will take care of one year of labor.
- Father, let favor open new doors of opportunities before me; let favor bring me before great men and women.
- Lord, I reject and remove from my life every aroma of disfavor and rejection.
- I confess I shall be the head and not the tail. I will walk in favor with God and men.

43. When You Need a Wife

Proverbs 18:22, Proverbs 12:4

- Thank you, Lord, for you are a perfect matchmaker and you know who is best for me.
- I receive your favor to find a good wife as you did for Adam.
- Father, I pray you will order our steps towards one another.
- Lord, give me the woman after your heart who will be a help-meet for me in life.
- Let my future wife be a God-fearing woman, a woman of character, a homemaker, and a pillar of support for my life.
- I pray against every spirit of error and confusion regarding this choice. I shall not make a mistake in the selection of my life partner.
- In the Name of Jesus, I reject a counterfeit wife, life-destroying woman, and a wife who will make my life miserable.
- Lord, grant me peace of mind and patience to wait for the manifestation of your perfect will for my life.
- I receive and embrace by faith the bone of my bones and the flesh of my flesh, according to your word.
- I declare and decree that there will be no delay or hindrance to the manifestation of the woman you have chosen for me.

44. When You Need a Husband

Proverbs 3:4, Psalm 37:23

- Thank you, Lord, for you are a perfect matchmaker and you know who is best for me.
- I receive your favor to find a good husband as you did for Eve and Rebecca.
- Father, I pray you will order our steps towards one another and reveal my husband to me.
- Lord, give me the man after your heart who will be a help-meet for me in life.
- Let my future husband be a God-fearing man, a man of integrity, a lover, and a pillar of support for my life.
- I pray against every spirit of error and confusion regarding this choice. I shall not make a mistake in the selection of my life partner.
- In the Name of Jesus, I reject counterfeit husband, a life wrecker, a man beater, and a husband who will make my life miserable.
- Lord, grant me peace of mind and patience to wait for the manifestation of your perfect will for my life.
- I receive and embrace by faith the bone of my bones and the flesh of my flesh, according to your word.
- I declare and decree that there will be no delay or hindrance to the manifestation of the man you have chosen for me.

45. When You Are Starting a New Business
Psalm 1:3, Isaiah 48:17

- Thank you, Lord, for the prospects of this new business you have given to me.

- Father, I ask that you bless my effort and place your hands on this business.

- Lord, I pray that you open the door of opportunity over this business and cause me to meet the right people.

- I declare that this business will not fail or enter into bankruptcy.

- Lord, teach my hands to profit and guide me in the way I should operate this business. Reveal to me hidden riches and connect me with the right partners.

- Heavenly Father, I ask for favor with God and with men over this business. Release helpers of destiny to come my way.

- According to your word, let everything I lay my hands upon prosper. Cause this business to flourish and prosper.

- Grant me the right location, give me the right contact. Release the resources needed for this business to come to my hands.

- Grant me the wisdom to operate this business. Lord, release unto me divine ideas and new initiatives that will make this business flourish.

- I decree and declare in the Name of the Lord, that every device and attack of the enemy against my business shall not succeed.

46. When You Are Persecuted

2 Corinthians 4:8-11, Matthew 5:10-12

- Father, arise to my defense, let all my accusers be ashamed.
- Lord, thwart the counsel of the aggressor, frustrate the plans of the evil one.
- I decree and declare that every trap and snare laid against me shall fail. I will not fall into the trap of my enemy.
- Jesus, I ask that you remove the spirit of hatred and animosity against my life.
- I receive your favor in my life. Remove the spirit of disfavor from me. Turn every hatred to love.
- In the Name of Jesus, I destroy the conspiracy of evil going on against me at work, in the family, from all my foes.
- Lord, give me divine strength, wisdom, and grace to handle every insult, attack, and animosity against my life.
- Protect my heart, Lord, from hatred. Help me to love my persecutors and pray for my enemies according to your word.
- Father, raise friends and strangers to speak on my behalf. Be my advocate, fight for me.
- I give you thanks for victory over my persecutors. I shall triumph over every attack.

47. When You Fail

Proverbs 24:16, Psalm 37:23-24, Jeremiah 29:11

- Lord, I thank you that failure is not final. In every situation, you are still good.
- I declare that I am not a failure. I will succeed.
- Lord, turn this failure around. Let something good come out of it.
- I refuse to be discouraged. Let your Holy Spirit give me comfort in this situation.
- Lord, reveal to me what went wrong. Show me what I missed and lead me to make the change needed to succeed.
- I ask for wisdom and strength to turn around this failure and help me to succeed. Direct me and instruct me on what I should do next.
- I declare that the Lord will restore to me what the cankerworm and locusts have eaten out of my life.
- I pray that the failure I face now will become an opportunity for outstanding success.
- I confess failure is not final, defeat is not fatal. I am a champion, not a failure. I shall arise out of this situation and give God glory.

48. Prayer for Your Husband

Proverbs 3:5-6, 4:20-23; Psalm 90:17

- Heavenly Father, I am grateful to you for my husband. Thank you for giving me a man after your heart.
- I pray that your hands will be on my husband and grant him wisdom and understanding to lead our family.
- I pray that my husband will be a great lover: a lover of God and our family.
- Lord, I pray that you will give my husband good health and remove from his life every form of disease and infirmity.
- Father, let my husband find your favor at his workplace or business and let him succeed in his career.
- I ask that you deliver him from temptation and evil. Protect him from every attack of the enemy. Let him not fall into the trap of the evil one.
- Father, I ask that you surround my husband with good friends and great counselors who will impact his life positively. Separate him from negative influences.
- I desire that you bless my husband financially as the provider for our home. Put resources into his hands and let him not lack for anything.
- Lord, help my husband to be a good father, an example to our children, a godly man who leads his family wisely.
- Bless my husband in every way to be a leader and example in our community, the church, and neighborhood.
- Deliver my husband from scandal. Protect him from lust and immorality. Make him to be strong in character.

49. Prayer for Your Wife

Proverbs 31, Psalm 128:3

- ⤞ Heavenly Father, I am grateful to you for my wife. Thank you for giving me a God-fearing woman.
- ⤞ I pray that your hands will be on my wife and grant her strength and grace to be a good wife and mother.
- ⤞ Lord, I pray that you will give my wife good health and remove from her life every form of disease and infirmity.
- ⤞ Father, let my wife find your favor at her workplace or business and let her succeed in her career.
- ⤞ I ask that you deliver her from temptation and evil. Protect her from every attack of the enemy. Let her not fall into the trap of the evil one.
- ⤞ Father, I ask that you surround my wife with good friends and great counselors who will impact her life positively. Separate her from negative influences.
- ⤞ Lord, help my wife to be a good mother, an example to our children, and a godly woman who cares for and supports her family.
- ⤞ Lord, I pray that you fill my wife with divine wisdom to handle whatever challenges come her way.
- ⤞ Lord, give her long life and good health to see her children's children.

50. Overcoming Tragedies

Lamentations 3:22-24, Romans 8:28, John 14:27

- Father, I give you thanks for your eternal love and care over me and my family.
- I ask you to grant me strength and grace to overcome this tragedy. Help me rise above it.
- Lord turn my ashes to beauty, turn this tragedy to a blessing in disguise.
- I declare this storm will not swallow me up, my faith will not drown because of this.
- O Lord, comfort my heart and bring forth your healing in this adversity and negative situation.
- Jesus, stand with me in this hour of difficulty; hold my hands steady and keep me strong.
- Lord, I put my trust in you. Let not the enemy prevail against me. Let those that seek my downfall be put to shame.
- I receive the wisdom to know what to do in this time of difficulty. I will not be overcome or defeated by this situation.
- Father, send the needed help to my soul. Send helpers of destiny to me and give me the solution to my adversity.
- I declare in the Name of Jesus that no weapon formed against me shall prosper. I overthrow the arrow of darkness sent to my soul.

51. When Facing Temptations

1 Corinthians 10:13, 2 Timothy 4:18

- ❧ Father, strengthen me against every temptation and trial in my life.

- ❧ I receive the grace and power to overcome every temptation that comes my way. Let me not fail in the time of temptations.

- ❧ Lord, surround me with your Holy Angels in the hour of temptations to strengthen and encourage me.

- ❧ Lord, make a way of escape for me to overcome every temptation and trial I face in my life.

- ❧ Jesus, work in me to will and do your good pleasure. Let the desire to please the Lord prevail in my life.

- ❧ I bind every demonic activity around my life. I overthrow the devices of the evil one and defeat his attacks against me.

- ❧ I give you thanks because your grace is sufficient for me in all the battles I face in life.

- ❧ Uphold my hands and keep my feet strong. Teach my hands to fight and my fingers to war and defeat the enemy of my soul.

- ❧ Deliver me, O Lord, from the traps of temptations. Open my eyes and ears to recognize when temptation is near.

52. When You Are Seeking to Know the Will of God

Psalm 32:8

- Show me your will, O God, lead me in the way I should go.
- Enlighten my darkness, remove confusion from my life.
- Open my ears, Lord, that I may hear you clearly and recognize your voice.
- Father, grant me a discerning spirit to know what you want me to do in the multitude of options.
- Hold my hands, Lord, let me not go astray. Let me not miss your plans and purpose for my life.
- Cause me to delight in doing your will for my life. Give me the spirit of obedience to follow your instructions.
- Holy Spirit, fill me, I pray, with your light. Reveal hidden things to me and show me the correct path to follow in life.
- I remove and rebuke every spirit of confusion, doubt, uncertainty, and dilemma in my life.
- I declare I will not be stranded in life. I will know the plans of God and I will follow them.

53. When You Are Struggling With Bad Habits and Addiction

John 8:36, 1 John 4:4, Philippians 4:13

- Father, break the controlling power of addiction over my life.
- Let the power of the Holy Spirit set me free from my bad habits.
- Lord, in the name of Jesus, I destroy the hold of the evil one over my life.
- I receive the strength and the enablement to say no when the temptation to yield comes on me.
- I cut off every evil association that encourages addiction in my life. Help me, Lord, to avoid the wrong environment that puts me in harm's way.
- Dear Lord, put a desire in my heart to love you and stay away from all controlling habits in my life. Help me to have a longing for your word.
- Father, place around my life people of good influence and solid character that will help me overcome my addiction.
- Lord, deliver me from every trap the enemy continues to set for my downfall. Grant me understanding and wisdom to know how to overcome.
- Let the shackles around my feet and chains that tied my hands be broken now. Let the veil that covered my eyes be broken.
- I receive my freedom today. I shall not be in bondage again. For whosoever the Son of God sets free shall be free indeed.

54. When You Are Making a Career Change
Isaiah 48:17, Psalm 32:8

- Holy Spirit, order my steps to the right place in life.
- Guide me and direct my ways that I will not make mistakes with my decisions.
- Show me, Lord, the fullness of your plan for my life, especially in my life career. Reveal to me where my blessings are.
- Teach my hands to profit, guide my fingers to prosper in life.
- Lord, send helpers of destiny to my life. Release people that will mentor me and help me fulfill my purpose.
- Bless the work of my hands, O Lord. Cause me to prosper in all my endeavors.
- Release into my life divine ideas to prosper. Anoint me with wisdom and creativity.
- Father, open new doors for me. Let great opportunities show up and bring me into divine breakthroughs in my career.
- Thank you, my Father, because I know you shall lead me and feed me.
- I declare and confess that I shall not be miserable in life. I shall not be abandoned.
- Cover me with your divine favor as I apply for new positions and attend interviews. I shall not be rejected.

55. When You Are Tired and Exhausted and Stressed Out

1 Corinthians 12:9, Isaiah 41:10, Isaiah 40:31

- Lord, you are worthy to be glorified and praised for all your kindness and strength in my life.
- I pray for renewal of my strength: physical, emotional, and spiritual.
- Father, I exchange my weakness for divine strength. Let there be a fresh infusion of energy into my life.
- I overcome every physical stress in my life. Lord, touch every fiber in my body; may my bones, flesh, and every organ receive supernatural strength right now.
- Breathe on me, Holy Spirit. Let fresh breath from the Lord flow into my life and remove stress and weakness.
- I reject every frustration that is responsible for stress in my life. I receive divine ability to manage my schedule and I eliminate whatever is sapping my energy.
- I confess and declare that the Lord is the strength of my life. I shall not be weary or stressed.
- As I wait upon the Lord, I renew my strength. I shall run and not be weary, I shall walk and not faint.
- I come against exhaustion, weariness, stress, frustrations, discouragement, and every arrow of weakness in my life.
- Lord, I obtain perfect rest in you. I rely upon you for divine strength. I depend on the Holy Spirit to assist me in all my deficiencies.
- I can do all things through Christ who strengthens me.

56. When You Need to Forgive
Ephesians 4:31-32, Matthew 6:12

- Lord, thank you for forgiving my sins and iniquities and for pardoning me of all my transgressions.
- I repent and apologize for every grudge, offense, and bitterness I have harbored in my heart.
- I receive your grace to release everyone who has offended me in the past. Lord, grant me the power to overlook every offense committed against me.
- Lord, through your help today, I wholeheartedly release and forgive everyone that has hurt and wronged me in any way.
- I start a clean slate, a fresh page for all my adversaries and offenders. I disallow hatred and anger in my heart.
- Dear forgiving Father, help me to find in my heart room to love those who have done me wrong. Enable me to forgive and forget their trespasses against me.
- From today, Lord, fill my heart with your perfect peace and joy. Replace every bitterness with love, every anger with compassion, and every pain with your peace.
- I cultivate from now on a heart free of offenses, a large heart filled with love and patience to relate with others.
- Father, I decree that every root of bitterness, malice, grudges, and anger be completely uprooted in my life along with every trace of animosity.
- I thank you for forgiving me and giving me the strength to forgive others. My prayers will not be hindered because I have released those who hurt me.

57. When You Are Seeking Wisdom
James 1:5, Proverbs 4:7

- ᛭ I give you thanks, my Father, because you are the author of wisdom. You are perfect in understanding and from you flows wisdom.

- ᛭ I desire from you today that you will grant unto me wisdom and understanding needed to make decisions.

- ᛭ Lord, grant unto me a heart full of discernment and excellence in wisdom to make wise choices.

- ᛭ Father, I ask that your wisdom will help me to overcome confusion, dilemma, and frustration in my life as I make correct decisions.

- ᛭ I refuse and reject every form of foolishness and stupidity in my life. I declare I will not make wrong turns and ungodly decisions.

- ᛭ I pray for wisdom in my finances, marriage, and in running my career and business.

- ᛭ Fill me now with the spirit of understanding that anytime I open my mouth to speak, your wisdom will pour out of me.

- ᛭ Lord, release in me the hunger for knowledge and wisdom. Take away from my life all devices of the evil one to rob me of God's wisdom from above.

- ᛭ Grant me a discerning and understanding heart to make quality decisions in life. Grant me the spirit of counsel to direct my paths.

- ᛭ Purge my lips and sanctify my mouth that wise pronouncements may proceed from it.

58. When You Are Seeking Guidance and Direction
Psalm 32:8

- I thank you, Lord, because you are my shepherd and guide.
- Lord, let your light shine on my path and lighten up my ways.
- I receive your guidance and direction for my life.
- Lord, show me the way I should go, lead me in the right direction.
- Holy Spirit, I ask that you order my steps and grant me counsel at this junction of my life.
- In Jesus' Name, I rebuke every spirit of confusion around my life.
- Lord, open my eyes to see what you want me to do right now.
- Teach me, O Lord. Give me your divine counsel that I may choose rightly.
- Father, take hold of my spirit, my feet, and my understanding, and reveal your perfect will for my life.
- I confess and declare that I will not be confused, I will not be misdirected, and I will not choose wrongly.

59. Prayer for Your Parents

Psalm 91:16, 128:6

- Lord, I thank you for the lives of my parents.
- Father, I speak strength into the lives of my parents.
- I declare you will keep and preserve their lives. Grant them long life.
- I pray that they will not be afflicted with sicknesses and infirmities. Heal them from every bodily affliction.
- Father, I pray that you will grant my parents joy and fulfillment in life over their children and the works of their hands.
- Let my parents reap to the fullest the blessings they have sown into other people's lives and those of their children.
- I pray that my parents will not mourn in life, they will be spared from sorrows. They will not bury their children.
- Lord, grant my parents to enjoy their retirements whenever they do.
- I pray that my parents will continually be filled with wisdom and understanding to guide their children in the right way.
- Lord, protect them from accidents in the air, on the road, or inside the house. They will not suffer bodily injury and no harm will come near them.

60. Prayer for Your Friends

Ephesians 3:14-20, 1 Thessalonians 3:12-13

- Lord, I give you thanks for the gift of friendship. Thank you for the people with whom you surround me.
- Lord, I pray for the peace and safety of all my friends.
- Father, protect them from evil, harm, hurts, and mishaps.
- In Jesus' Name, I desire that you will meet their individual needs (physical, emotional, financial, and spiritual).
- Today, I ask for all my friends to be blessed in all their undertakings. Grant them their heart desires.
- I pray, Father, that the love and care that exist between me and my friends shall continue to grow and flourish.
- I declare against the spirit of confusion, misunderstanding, and strife. Peace and harmony will continue to reign in our friendships.
- Lord, bless my friends' careers and jobs. Let them continue to excel and prosper.
- Lord, fill my friends with divine wisdom and guide them in all their endeavors.
- Dear Lord, show my friends your salvation and cause them to know and love you.
- Lord, be with their families and loved ones. Let them all fulfill their purposes on earth.

61. When You Feel Discouraged and Want to Give Up

Joshua 1:9, Isaiah 41:10

- In the Name of Jesus, I refuse to quit, give up, or surrender to defeat in my life.
- I declare I am strong and courageous. I am not a quitter but a winner. I am not a victim but a champion.
- In the Name of Jesus, I defeat the demons of discouragement working against me and I root out every tool the enemy is using to distract me from attaining success.
- I rise up above discouragement today, I refuse to allow the enemy to make me quit.
- Father, release to my life the Spirit of encouragement and reassurance of your presence in my life.
- Grant me the tenacity needed to hold on to the end. Fortify me in my spirit to be strong and confident in your promises.
- I refuse to be afraid; I judge the spirit of fear in my life. I rebuke the spirit of incompletion to release its hold over my life.
- I confess that I shall complete what I started, I shall arrive at my destination and I will successfully run my race to the end.
- Lord, help me to hold on and keep my eyes on you and not my distractors. Help me not lose heart when times are rough and difficult.
- I give you thanks for your promises never to leave me or forsake me (Hebrews 13:5). I trust you to see me through to the end.

62. When You Are Facing Danger
Job 5:19

- ᛫᛫᛭ Thank you, Lord, for your protection and safety over my life.

- ᛫᛫᛭ Lord, I pray that you will deliver me from the impending dangers around me.

- ᛫᛫᛭ Father, I hide myself in the Name of Jesus, which is a Hightower.

- ᛫᛫᛭ Heavenly Father, I pray that you will deliver me from every snare and trap of the evil one set against my life.

- ᛫᛫᛭ In the Name of the Lord Jesus, I dismantle every satanic plan and evil conspiracy against my life.

- ᛫᛫᛭ I declare and decree no weapon fashioned against me shall prosper. I condemn every tongue that rises against me.

- ᛫᛫᛭ Lord, I pray that you will cover me with the precious blood of Jesus. I speak the blood over my life.

- ᛫᛫᛭ In Jesus' Name, I draw the blood line around my properties, my house, my family, and all that pertains to me. No evil shall prevail over me.

- ᛫᛫᛭ Lord, dispatch your angels to surround me and protect me from dangers. I shall not dash my feet against stones.

- ᛫᛫᛭ I destroy, in the Name of Jesus, every arrow of wickedness. I nullify every weapon; I command the devices of the wicked one be destroyed in my life.

- ᛫᛫᛭ I rebuke and reject the spirit of fear, anxiety, and panic around my life. I refuse to be intimidated by the harassment of the devil.

63. When You Are in Spiritual Bondage

Isaiah 49:24-26, Numbers 23:23

- Lord, I confess and repent from every sin and iniquity in my life through which the enemy put me in bondage. Forgive me and cleanse me from every transgression.
- Father, in the Name of Jesus, deliver me from every bondage around my life.
- Lord, set me free from every manner of oppression of the evil one.
- I declare my liberty in the Name of Jesus from every spiritual affliction.
- In the mighty Name of Jesus, I break every fetter and chain of bad habits, wrong thoughts, and emotional manipulation of the enemy in my life.
- I renounce and reject every enchantment, spell, voodoo, and evil pronouncement against my life.
- Lord, let the fire of the Holy Spirit devour and destroy all manners of evil bondage in my physical, emotional, and spiritual life.
- I close every doorway through which affliction and oppression gain access into my life by the blood of Jesus.
- I confess and declare the greater One is inside of me. He that is in me is greater than he that is against me.
- Lord, fight for me, let the power of the blood prevail on my behalf.
- Lord, I pray that you teach my hands to fight and my fingers to war against every spiritual battle arrayed against me.

64. When You Are Perplexed and Overwhelmed
Psalm 27:1, 61:1

- Thank you, Lord, because you are my strength and my help.

- Father, I confess and declare that I can do all things through Christ who strengthens me.

- Lord, I receive grace and ability to handle everything that comes my way. Place your hands over me and help me through every challenge.

- I take a stand against the spirit of discouragement in my life. I cast out the spirit of fear and perplexity.

- Lord, uphold me by your hands of righteousness, strengthen me in my weakness, and grant me divine ability.

- Heavenly Father, I pray that you will help me to overcome weariness, tiredness, and burnout. Refresh me and renew me physically.

- Lord, release to my life true rest and peace of God. Grant me serenity in all my endeavors.

- I confess and declare you are my strength, my hiding place in times of trouble, and the lifter up of my head in a time like this when I feel overwhelmed.

- I receive direction and spiritual discretion to know what I should do right now and to recognize what the priorities are.

- Lord, I command the mountains of challenges causing me to feel overwhelmed to be dismantled right now in Jesus' Name.

65. When Marking Your Birthday

Jeremiah 29:11, Psalm 20:4, 145:19

- ᛞ Lord, I give you glory and express my appreciation to you for adding another year to my life.

- ᛞ Father, I am very grateful for your love, care, and provisions for me for all the years I have lived on earth.

- ᛞ I desire of you, Father, that you will make this new year a new beginning and fresh start for me.

- ᛞ Holy Spirit, fill me with wisdom and understanding commensurate with my age.

- ᛞ Lord, grant me strength and good health to enjoy the rest of my days on earth.

- ᛞ I decree and declare that every evil plan of the enemy over my life shall be thwarted.

- ᛞ Lord, open new doors before me, grant me new opportunities in life.

- ᛞ Let the rest of my life be better and more pleasant than the past.

- ᛞ Father, I desire that you grant me joy and fulfillment in my life.

- ᛞ I desire today a blessing and gift from you as my Maker and Creator on my birthday.

- ᛞ Jesus, I pray that you will keep me in safety and protect me for another year.

66. When Your Faith Is Weak

Luke 17:5, 2 Corinthians 12:8-10

- Oh Lord, I confess my weakness to you right now. I give you thanks because you are my helper.

- Heavenly Father, I challenge every weakness in my life and come against the spirit of doubt in the Name of Jesus.

- I proclaim that greater is He that is in me than he that is in the world.

- Jesus, I pray that you will strengthen my faith in your word and the promises of God given to me through your word.

- I take my eyes from every negative circumstance that is crushing my faith. I refuse to listen to the voice of the enemy in my life.

- I declare my faith will not sink. I will not go down in my walk with God.

- Lord, destroy every arrow of the enemy directed against my faith right now. Boost my faith and help me to overcome.

- I declare I am a victor and not a victim over every situation. I declare and proclaim my victory right now. This is the victory that overcome the world, even my faith.

- Lord, I set my face on you in every situation. I shall not be ashamed. My expectations shall not be defeated.

- Lord, turn the current situation into a testimony for me, bring beauty out of the ashes and glorify your name in my life.

- I give you thanks because I shall prevail, and I will not go down. I confess my faith is strong and not weak.

67. When Facing Discrimination

Psalm 94:1-4, 2 Samuel 22:48-49

- Hear my cry, O Lord, and avenge my cause.
- Lord, disappoint all my adversaries, let their plans against my life fail.
- Father, remove from me the spirit of hatred that is making people discriminate against me.
- I pray that you will cover me right now with your favor and place your glory over me.
- Lord, turn everyone that is against me into a friend. Touch their hearts on my behalf.
- I beseech you, O Lord, let every plot and conspiracy against my life become futile.
- I arrest right now every backbiting and gossiping tongue speaking evil against me.
- Lord, arise and raise up people to speak in my favor. Father, defend my course and be the voice for me where I have no voice.
- I overcome discrimination around me, at my workplace, in my relationship, and everywhere I go.
- Lord, shield me from the wrath of men and deliver me from evil set up.

68. When Your Relationship Fails and Falls Apart

Psalm 28:7, Isaiah 41:10

- The Lord is my helper and sustainer. You are my friend until the end of time.

- Father, I look up to you in this difficult time of my life for support and encouragement.

- Lord, reveal to me where I am wrong and give me the courage to make the necessary corrections.

- Father, stretch out your hands and keep me from falling and failing. Help me to pull through.

- I pray for your healing power to flow into my relationship right now. I ask for the grace of restoration.

- Jesus, I ask for the spirit of reconciliation between me and _____. Touch our hearts and bring your peace in a difficult time.

- Grant me and _____ the spirit of understanding of each other. Help us to get back on track.

- In the Name of Jesus, I pull down every wall of division, barrier, and differences that are currently prevailing in my relationship.

- Let your will be done in our lives as we realize our errors and make effort to make amends.

- I receive grace and wisdom to handle every difficulty and challenge that is associated with this relationship.

- I give you thanks for restoration, reconciliation, and healing.

69. When You Need Peace
John 14:27, Isaiah 54:10

- ❖ Lord, I thank you because you are my peace and the source of my joy. Without you, I am nothing.
- ❖ Lord, let not the covenant of your peace be removed from my life. Let your peace return fully.
- ❖ I stand in the Name of Jesus against every attempt of the devil to steal my peace away.
- ❖ Father, I receive from you peace with God, with men, and with myself.
- ❖ I command the peace of God that passes all understanding to flood my soul and mind.
- ❖ I claim your peace in my body against every form of bodily attack and injury.
- ❖ I receive your peace when I go to bed. You will grant me blessed rest in my sleep.
- ❖ I stop in their tracks every enemy of peace: worry, fear, anger, and any other thing trying to rob me of my peace.
- ❖ I ask for financial peace, marital peace, and career peace.
- ❖ Let the Prince of Peace Himself take absolute control of every faculty in my life.

70. When You Need Salvation

Romans 10:9, 13; Ephesians 2:8

- Lord, I repent of my sins. I am sorry for my disobedience and transgressions.

- Forgive me my sins, errors, shortcomings, and iniquities. Cleanse me, Lord, by the blood of Jesus.

- Lord, I invite you now into my heart. I ask you to be my Lord and Savior. Make me your child today.

- Jesus, I believe in my heart that you died to pay for my sins at the cross of Calvary. I recognize that I am lost without you.

- Holy Spirit, come right in and dwell in me. Give me the power to live as a child of God.

- I renounce my sins and disengage myself from my old ways of living. I reject the power of the evil one over my life and embrace Christ in my life.

- Lord, deliver me from every entanglement of sin, free me from slavery to my sinful nature and turn me around.

- Create in me a new heart, O Lord, renew the right spirit within me. Write my name in the book of life.

- Draw me closer to you; put a hunger for you in my heart. Remove the desire and hunger for sin from my heart and replace it with a thirst for righteousness.

- Father, raise for me a spiritual family that will care for me and help me to grow in you.

- Hold me, Lord, with your right hand of righteousness and keep my feet steady in you.

71. When You Just Had a Baby

Isaiah 40:29-31, 41:10

- Thank you, Father, for children are the heritage of the Lord.
- I am grateful for the safe delivery of this child. Thank you, Lord, for the gift of life.
- I cover this child under the precious blood of Jesus. I secure a glorious destiny for him/her.
- I receive perfect healing and good health for myself. I shall not experience postpartum afflictions and sicknesses.
- Lord, release to me the strength to nourish this child both physically, emotionally, and spiritually.
- I pray that I will not be anxious, weak, or emotionally down after childbirth.
- I pray, Lord, that you will send me all the help I need this time to raise this child both in physical support and in finances.
- Lord, keep my child strong and healthy and let him/her grow perfectly.
- I pray this child shall be free from all manner of childhood diseases and shall be free of problems.
- Let your peace surround this child, let your angels watch continually over him/her. Let no wicked or evil come near this baby.

72. Prayer for Infants and Newborns
Psalm 127:3-4

- Lord, thank you for the arrival of this new addition to our family.

- I pray that the arrival of this child shall be the beginning of peace, love, unity, and harmony in our family.

- I decree and declare the peace of God around this baby. There shall not be any sickness or affliction around him/her.

- I completely sanctify the atmosphere around this child: the air he/she breathes, the water and the food he/she eats, and every hand that carries this baby.

- I prophesy that this child shall be great in life. I speak to his/her destiny that his/her future shall be beautiful.

- Father, let your holy angels watch day and night over this baby. He/she shall not suffer any attack or sickness.

- Lord, I pray for wisdom and understanding to raise this child in the fear of God. I ask that this child shall grow to be a blessing to many and a vessel of grace in the community.

- Lord, I pray that you will lay your hands on this child and let him/her be a loving, God-fearing, diligent, and obedient child.

- I decree and declare in the Name of Jesus that no weapon of the enemy fashioned against this baby shall prosper.

- Lord, I pray for other infants in the world today, please protect them and preserve their lives.

73. When You Need Comfort
Isaiah 40:1, 51:3, 12; John 14:16

- Father, I thank you because you are the God of all comfort.
- Holy Spirit, you are my Comforter. Bring your comfort right now into my life.
- In Jesus' Name, I rebuke the spirit of heaviness and sorrow and I command it to take its leave out of my life.
- I confess and declare in the name of the Lord that I am free from depression, I am free from sadness and sorrow.
- I declare and confess that the joy of the Lord is my strength. I exchange now the spirit of heaviness for the garment of praise.
- Heavenly Father, calm my fearful heart, take the pain from my heart and replace it with your presence.
- Jesus, I exchange my weakness for your strength. Release your supernatural peace into my heart and let your voice bring me comfort.
- Let your oil of joy and gladness become a living spring and flow within me continually and wash away my sadness and sorrow.
- Heal me, O Lord, from broken heartedness. Restore unto me again my joy of salvation and renew a right spirit within me.

74. When in Courtship
Genesis 2:18, 2 Timothy 2:22, 1 Thessalonians 5:23

- I give thanks to you, Lord, for blessing me with a suitable partner.
- Let my partner be a source of blessing and inspiration to my life.
- Lord, I pray that you will bless our relationship with your presence and guide us continually.
- Father, remove every stumbling block out of our way, let there be no room for misunderstanding and quarrels.
- Lord, let my partner and I grow in our love and godly affection for one another. Let your peace reign and abide with us.
- I pray that you will sanctify us wholly: spirit, soul, and body. Remove far from us all manner of filthiness of the soul and body.
- Lord, teach us how to prepare for our future. Show us your plans and purpose for our lives.
- Lord, deliver us from temptations and every trap and impediment Satan may put on our path. Help us to be vigilant and alert to recognize his wiles.
- Heavenly Father, as we prepare for our wedding, I pray that you will give us divine provision and supply all our needs.
- I pray that you will keep us from evil and protect us from dangers in all our travels.

75. When Starting a New Job
Psalm 5:12, Psalm 102:13

- Lord, I am very grateful, and I give you thanks for a new job.
- Lord, prepare me soul, spirit, and body for this new job. Let me be in the right spirit.
- I pray that you will remove all obstacles out of my way that may prevent me from success.
- Father, release your favor on me. Let me obtain it in the sight of my boss and associates.
- Bless me with confidence and grant me boldness to do my job effectively. Make me strong in the spirit.
- I reject the spirit of fear and intimidation. I will not be harassed, embarrassed, or molested on the job.
- Lord, let your supernatural wisdom flow into my life. I will act with godly wisdom and display the spirit of excellence on the job.
- I pray that a cordial relationship will blossom between me and my colleagues at work. There will be no room for animosity, envy, or hatred.
- Lord, cause me to find fulfillment in my new job. Let it not become monotonous and boring.
- Help me, Lord, to shine for you and be a good example in my new job.

76. When There Is a National Disaster

Jeremiah 33:6, Joel 2:15

- ❖ Father, we repent on behalf of our nation, and we ask for your forgiveness. We ask you to help us live in peace and safety.

- ❖ Lord, forgive us for bloodshed, ungodliness, evil, robberies, murders, immorality, violence, and all the vices that are ravaging our nation. Protect us from destruction.

- ❖ We turn to you for your mercy, and we plead for your intervention in our nation.

- ❖ We pray for the healing of this land, O Lord. Heal our societies and our families and restore your peace.

- ❖ Lord, we come against the power of darkness working in the lives of our young people in the form of violence, drugs, and immorality.

- ❖ Prince of Peace, we seek your peace over every family and community at war against one another.

- ❖ We come against diseases and afflictions ravaging our land. We stop them in their tracks. Remove the plague of infections and epidemics.

- ❖ We wage war against vices of kidnappings, abductions, assassinations, murders, gun violence, and the evil destroying our society.

- ❖ We pray against hurricanes, tornadoes, violent storms, floods, earthquakes, and other natural disasters that are destroying our homes and the lives of our people.

- ❖ Lord, protect our nation against terrorism, vandalism, and other violent acts that rob people's lives.

77. When Relocating or Moving to a New House
Isaiah 32:18, 2 Samuel 7:29, 2 Chronicles 7:15-16

- Thank you, Father, for your wisdom and counsel regarding my life.
- I pray for the spirit of guidance and direction to come upon me and show me what to do.
- Lord, order my steps aright. Let me not miss your will and purpose in every decision I make.
- I dedicate and sanctify this new house in the Name of Jesus and cover it with the precious blood of Jesus.
- Lord, I receive your perfect peace in the new location, I shall not encounter any form of evil.
- Let the angels of the Lord encamp round about the new house; let the eyes of the Lord be all over it.
- I ask for your protection and safety during the transition. I shall not encounter any harm or accident.
- In Jesus' Name, I uproot and remove every evil within and without the house that has been operating in the area before my arrival.
- Thank you, Lord, for this relocation. May this transition be peaceful, joyful, and rewarding for me and my family.
- May I not regret my decision to relocate and move. May I not relocate into troubles and disasters.

78. When Dealing with Disability
2 Corinthians 12:9, Psalm 121

- Lord, you are my strength and my healer. I declare you are my helper when I am weak.

- Lord, be merciful unto me at this period of life. Let your grace be sufficient for me.

- Send unto me helpers of destiny to provide the needed support at this stage of life.

- Father, I receive your spirit of encouragement in my life. I shall not be discouraged or depressed.

- Give me strength in my inner man, emotions, and physical abilities.

- Grant me the serenity to go through this and come out of it on top.

- I ask for your healing power to go through my body, my soul, and my mind. I receive the touch of your hands in my life.

- Lord, by your grace, help me to overcome the barriers and limitations resulting from this disability.

- I give you the glory that your presence abides with me in all my difficulties. You promised never to leave me or abandon me.

- I refuse to sink in self-pity, dejection, and rejection. I declare I am a victor and not a victim. I can do all things through your strength in me.

79. When You Are in an Accident
Psalm 118:17, 121:7

- Thank you, Lord, for sparing my life from death. This could have been worse.

- Lord, I am grateful for releasing your angels to rescue me from sudden destruction.

- Lord, I pray that you stretch your hands right now to touch every part of my body that is hurting.

- Lord, let there be no complication resulting from this accident. I will not have permanent injury.

- I pray for your hands to touch and help everyone (if any) involved with me in this accident.

- I cover my life from the crown of my head to the sole of my feet with the blood of Jesus.

- I shall not die but live to declare the glory of God in my life.

- Lord, I cancel every evil plan and agenda of the devil regarding my life. The plan of the wicked one will not prosper in my life.

- Send my way right now the right help to assist me in the hospital and at home. Reveal every hidden injury and bring forth your healing.

- I give thanks for my quick recovery from this accident and healing from every injury I might have sustained.

80. When You Make a Costly Mistake

Romans 8:28, 2 Thessalonians 2:17

- ↦ Thank you, Father, because of your love and mercy continually towards me.

- ↦ Lord, I ask for your forgiveness for every form of mistake, carelessness, and negligence on my part.

- ↦ Father, I pray that your mercy and compassion will give me grace to reverse this error and mistake of my life.

- ↦ I pray that your hands of grace will contain and curtail the implications of my mistakes in my life and the lives of other people.

- ↦ I plead that your divine intervention will turn my mistake and mess around and bring a miracle out of it.

- ↦ Lord, I pray that you will open my eyes to see what I missed. Grant me the wisdom to realize what went wrong.

- ↦ I declare that the devil will not have room to manipulate and amplify my mistakes to destroy my future and the lives of other people.

- ↦ Give me the grace, the strength, and the courage to rise out of the mistakes I have made. I refuse to allow this mistake of my life to bury me and destroy my potentials.

- ↦ I give you thanks because you are the Alpha and the Omega of my life, and you are able to bring opportunities in the midst of my adversities.

- ↦ Give me a second chance to testify to your goodness in spite of this situation.

81. When You Need a Miracle or a Breakthrough
Genesis 18:14, Jeremiah 32:27

- Father, there is nothing too hard for you. Nothing is impossible for you to do.
- Dear God, I position myself for divine intervention in my life. I trust you for a turn around right now of my situation.
- Lord, my eyes are on you, let me not be put to shame in life.
- Turn every hopeless situation around and give me a testimony.
- Give me an "Isaac" in my difficult situation, put laughter in my mouth. Turn my mourning into laughter again.
- Lord, turn my midnight crisis to a miracle. Step up and stand up for me in this situation. Let your mighty hands turn things around.
- I command in the Name of Jesus that this negative situation shall bow to the authority of Jesus. I destroy every resistance in the path of my miracle.
- Lord, raise people up from different corners of the world to assist me. Use people I don't know to give me the breakthrough I desperately need.
- Father, turn my tests to testimonies, turn my trials to triumphs, and turn my stumbling blocks to stepping stones of breakthrough.
- I confess and declare in the Name of the Lord that I shall overcome and testify to the goodness of the Lord in this situation.

82. When You Just Graduate or for Your Graduate Children or Friends

Psalm 37:37, Proverbs 4:18

- Lord, I give you thanks for the grace of completion in my life or _____'s life.

- I declare the spirit of success and progress over my life continually.

- Lord, let me never be backward in life. Help me to go forward and very far in life.

- I pray and receive my miracle job following my graduation. Open new prospects for me.

- I ask for divine favor to follow me wherever I go. I shall be preferred and chosen among many.

- Dear Lord, I ask for the spirit of excellence to follow me in life. Let an excellent spirit be over the works of my hands.

- I pray that you will give me credible relationships and bring good people along my path. Release into my life helpers of destiny.

- Lord, let my path shine brighter and brighter into a perfect day. Let your light guide my steps.

- Father, I pray for divine guidance as I make vital decisions about my future and career. Let me not go astray or choose wrongly.

- Lord, prosper my way, bless the works of my hands, and fill my life with joy. Let not my expectations in life be cut off.

83. When You Are Pregnant

Exodus 1:19, Isaiah 66:9

- Father, I give you thanks for my pregnancy. Thank you for your blessing in my life.
- I believe you who brought me to the place of conception will also sustain me throughout this pregnancy.
- Father, I receive the strength to carry my baby to term. I will not become sick or weak along the way.
- In Jesus' Name, I declare that I will overcome every form of sickness, symptoms, and challenges associated with early pregnancy.
- Let your hands be upon me and the baby inside of me. There shall not be any abnormality in its development.
- I declare I will not experience unwanted bleeding. I will not experience miscarriage in any form.
- Father, deliver me from every form of mishap, accident, or attack throughout my pregnancy.
- Let me experience your perfect peace in my body and my spirit throughout the pregnancy. I shall not need emergency hospitalization.
- I pray that my delivery will be peaceful and free of any form of complications. I will not lose too much blood or water. The labor will be calm and normal.
- I pray against evil arrows of wickedness in every form that may attack me or my baby throughout the period of my pregnancy.

84. When You Need Victory in Battles

Exodus 15:3, 2 Chronicles 20:17, Galatians 6:17

- I declare, "I am marked as untouchable. Let nobody, demons, or whoever trouble me."

- I raise the standard of the blood against impending dangers and troubles over my household. I draw the blood line over my property.

- I frustrate the plans and tokens of the enemy against my life. I take a stand against every demonic aggression in the name of the Lord.

- I put a wall of defense and shield of protection from the arrows of the wicked over my life and family.

- Father, I declare over my life that the siege of the enemy be broken and the trap of the wicked be destroyed.

- I confess and declare Psalm 27:5 over my life: "For in the time of trouble he shall hide me in his pavilion: in the secret of his tabernacle shall he hide me; he shall set me up upon a rock."

- I declare Job 5:19 over my life and family: "He shall deliver thee in six troubles: yea, in seven there shall no evil touch thee."

- I ask the Lord to fight my battles for me as the Captain of the Host of my army. I will never be ashamed nor confounded.

- I pray that the Lord will overturn the table of the wicked and give me a testimony out of the desperate situation.

- I confess Isaiah 50:7: "For the Lord GOD will help me; therefore shall I not be confounded: therefore have I set my face like a flint, and I know that I shall not be ashamed."

85. When You Need Confidence
2 Timothy 1:7, Hebrews 10:35

- Lord, I confess you have not given me the spirit of fear but of power, love, and sound mind.

- I rebuke and reject the spirit of fear, intimidation, and harassment in my life.

- Father, fill me with courage and confidence in my life. Help me to appreciate who I am and what you have done for me.

- In the Name of Jesus, I come against low self-esteem, inferiority complex, and every negative thought that tends to put me down.

- I confess and declare that I am what God says I am and I can do what God says I can. I can do all things through Christ who strengthens me.

- I receive the confidence I need right now in the Name of the Lord to face every adversary, the next project, and the assignment in front of me.

- I shall overcome every Goliath in my way. I shall cross every Red Sea in my path and I will climb every mountain that seems impossible.

- Psalm 27:1: The Lord is my light and my salvation; whom shall I fear? The Lord is the strength of my life; of whom shall I be afraid?

- Father, let the Holy Spirit strengthen me within and grant unto me the spirit of boldness and confidence.

- Let me feel your abiding presence around me; reveal your power in me.

86. When Entering a New Year
Isaiah 40:4-5, Hebrews 13:5-6

- Lord, I am grateful for another year that I just witnessed. Thank you for keeping me alive.

- I receive your presence to go with me throughout this New Year. I shall not experience misfortune in my life.

- I ask for divine direction and guidance for every step and decision I shall make this year. You will guide me to your blessings.

- Father, I ask that you unfold your plans for me and grant the desires of my heart.

- Every ugly phase and chapter of my life, family, job, business, ministry, and career in the previous year shall be clothed and decorated like the beauty of the rainbow this year.

- I shall experience a season of abundance in my life as I enter this year. Every drought and lack shall be gone.

- I decree and declare that I shall not experience premature death in my life and family this year. You shall deliver us from evil and keep us as the apple of your eyes.

- This shall be a year of favor in my life. I shall be at the right place at the right time with the right people.

- I declare I will make progress this year; I will not be stuck or stagnated in any area of my life. I shall move forward, and things shall be fast for me.

- Your goodness and mercy shall follow me throughout this year. Whatever I lay my hands on shall prosper. I shall thrive in every area of life.

87. When You Are in Conflict
1 Corinthians 14:33, James 3:13-18

- Lord, I receive clear instructions from you on how to handle this conflict.

- Lord, deliver me from the spirit of strife and fault finding in my relationships and associations.

- I overcome every plan of the enemy to make me miss or lose my blessings through conflict and strife.

- I receive your peace all around my life, my family, my workplace, and in the church.

- I reject right now the spirit of animosity, rejection, and division operating around my vicinity. I command their power to be neutralized.

- Dear Lord, bring clarity where confusion reigns, bring peace where there is division, and grant serenity in the atmosphere of strife.

- Lord, help me to be a peacemaker, a lover of peace, and a defender of truth.

- Give me wisdom to manage every situation spinning out of control. I receive the patience needed to resolve every conflict.

- In the Name of Jesus, I arrest now every spirit behind this conflict, confusion, and division. Open the eyes of all the parties to see the truth.

- Thank you, Lord, for you are the Prince of Peace and wherever you are your peace reigns. I invoke the presence of the Prince of Peace right now.

88. When You Are Facing Delays

Psalm 138:8, Jeremiah 1:12

- Heavenly Father, thank you because I believe delay is not denial. I thank you because you are in perfect control of my life.

- Lord, I come against every form of discouragement and despair in my life. I refuse to give up in defeat.

- Holy Spirit, grant me grace to patiently wait on you and not become frantic and impatient.

- In the Name of the Lord, I rebuke every form of demonic delay in my life, and I declare every obstacle standing in my path be removed.

- Lord, let your mighty Hands hasten the manifestation of my blessings and breakthrough. Speed up the process for manifestations.

- In the Name of Jesus, I rebuke the "Prince of Persia" causing delay in the manifestations of my prayers.

- Send your Angel warrior to arise and fight for me. Let the victory be released now on my behalf.

- I declare and confess my victory. I shall prevail over this situation and shall not be defeated.

- Father, I depend on you for the final outcome. I refuse to quit or bow out in hopelessness.

- I pray, dear Lord, to finish what you have begun in my life and bring to completion your good work over me. Take me to the finish line.

89. When You Have Bad Dreams or Nightmares

Jeremiah 1:19, Isaiah 8:9-10

- Thank you, Lord, because the victory is mine. You are on my side and you fight for me.

- Lord, I pray for every attack and oppression in my dreams to stop with immediate effect.

- I nullify and reverse every bad dream and negative revelation I have lately. They shall not come to pass.

- I plead the blood of Jesus over my spirit, soul, and body, and I declare no weapon that is formed against me shall prosper.

- I speak to the future and pray that all shall be well and the power of God shall prevail.

- I refuse the spirit of fear and anxiety in every way that the enemy is trying to attack my heart. I shall not be afraid.

- I confess by faith that greater is He that is in me than the one that is in the world. God is for me; I shall not be moved.

- I blot all the handwriting of the wicked against my life and every evil force threatening me with nightmares. The covenant shall defend me and protect me.

- Dear Lord, protect me from the power of darkness in my dream and deliver me from the arrows of the wicked.

- I return every arrow to its sender. I overcome the power of the wicked bringing attacks in my dreams.

- Thank you, Lord, because I am victorious. I refuse to be controlled by my dreams or live in fear.

90. When You Are Stagnated and Need Promotion

Psalm 3:3, Psalm 75:6

- Jehovah Roi, The Lord who sees me, have mercy on me and my situation.
- Help me to see where I am stuck and why. Reveal to me the forces behind my stagnation.
- Open my eyes to see what steps to take to move forward.
- Grant me helpers of destiny that can provide opportunities for me to fulfill my purpose in life.
- Increase my faith in you, O Lord. I believe nothing is impossible for you to do.
- Give me a growth mindset so I will not be afraid of trying again.
- Open your heavens upon me, O Lord, and smile upon me once more. Let the earth yield her increase for me and bring me progress in every area of my career and life.
- Let your face shine upon me and grant me the desires of my heart according to your will.
- Give me the courage to develop myself in areas where I may be deficient. Release mentors into my life to take me to the next level of my growth.
- Increase my capacity to grow into the new role you have prepared for me.

91. When You Are in the Middle of a Crisis
Isaiah 54:4, 50:7; Daniel 6:21-22

- ❖ Help me to experience your presence right now, O Lord.
- ❖ You are my help; Lord, please deliver me from this situation even as you delivered Daniel from the lions' den.
- ❖ Grant me direction and the ability to see my way through this situation. Show me a way of escape that you have already made.
- ❖ Deliver me from the temptation to blame somebody else for this situation or make excuses.
- ❖ Make haste to help me, Lord. You are my light and salvation. Do not delay your divine intervention in my life; send your help and rescue my soul.
- ❖ In the Name of the Lord, I speak to this crisis to cease and desist. I command peace to return now.
- ❖ Have mercy on me, Lord. If I brought this upon myself, grant me the humility to accept responsibility for my actions.
- ❖ Order my steps in your word, O Lord, let me not go astray. Deliver me from wrong alternatives the enemy may create to derail me from your will.
- ❖ Thank you, Lord, for delivering me from evil. Let affliction not rise again a second time.
- ❖ Grant me peace of mind so I can hear you in the midst of this storm.

92. Prayer for Your Pastor

Ephesians 1:17-20, Ezekiel 3:8-9, Mark 16:17, 20

- Lord, grant my pastor continued refreshing in your presence. Remove from my pastor all factors that bring stress.
- Lord, help my pastor to increase in anointing to teach, direct, counsel, minister, and lead your people.
- Deliver my pastor from manipulations of evil men and women.
- Surround my pastor with God-fearing, hardworking, and mature associates who will truly stand by his/her side through the thick and thin.
- Father, send help to the pastor as your work grows in his/her hands.
- Grant the pastor wisdom as he/she manages situations that arise in the body of Christ.
- Lord, please give my pastor strength and peace of mind to carry burdens for the flock.
- Help my pastor to remain steadfast in the midst of challenges and difficulties.
- Enlarge his/her capacity to cope with any situation that arises in the body of Christ.
- Increase his/her ability to detect problems way ahead of time and squelch them before they build.

93. Prayer for Troubled and Difficult Children
1 Samuel 2:12, Proverbs 22:15, Psalm 119:9

- Thank you for the blessing of children.
- Lord, help me to be a good role model for my child and become a godly example to be followed.
- Lord, teach my child to love and respect your word. Let him/her not depart from the path of righteousness and godliness.
- Help him/her be a doer of the Word and not a hearer only. Let the light of your word shine in his/her path.
- Lord, deliver my child from the negative influence of peer pressure.
- Help him/her form opinions about life from the Word of God and godly counsels.
- Lord, help my child to experience the world through your eyes and not run with the wrong crowd.
- Lord, give my child the wisdom to make good choices.
- Lord, please let my child trust and come to me or a respected God-fearing leader when questions or problems arise.
- Heavenly Father, please deliver my child from the evil of this world and preserve him/her from the decadence of society.

94. When You Cannot Sleep
Psalm 3:5, Psalm 127: 2

- Thank you, Lord, for this week. Thank you, Lord, that you are always in control.
- I decree and declare that every attack of the enemy against my mind cease right now. I free myself from bombardments in my thoughts.
- Help me, Lord, not to worry about the situations around me at this time. I completely release my cares and concerns to your able hands, my Father, and I trust you are capable of handling them all.
- I release myself from fear, panic attack, anxiety, and the cares of my situation. Help me to remember that worrying does not change anything.
- Grant calmness and peace on my mind, emotions, and body. Let your peace flow over my soul.
- I receive rest unto my being in Jesus' Name.
- Help me to have a good rest and sleep. Help me to sleep like a baby in your arms.
- Help me to feel refreshed and recharged when awakened. Let my physical and spiritual energy be revitalized.
- Help me, Lord, to respect good sleep hygiene and to maintain physical and spiritual disciplines in my life.
- Thank you, Lord, because you give your beloved sweet sleep.

95. When You Are Anxious or Worried
Psalm 55:22, Philippians 4:6

- Dear Lord, help me not to fear. You foul spirit of fear, I command you in Jesus' Name to lose your hold from my life.
- Give me peace in my heart and mind and my body.
- Help me to remember that you are always in control.
- Thank you because all things work together for good and for those who are called according to your purpose.
- Holy Spirit, I invite you to be the guard over my mind and eliminate every unwanted thought that wants to put me in bondage.
- Thank you, Lord, because you have not given me the spirit of fear but of power, love, and a sound mind.
- I receive soundness in my mind, thoughts, and emotions. I declare that I am walking in authority and dominion; nothing shall move me.
- I receive the power to be calm. I confess my victory over the spirit of anxiety, fear, cares, and panic mode.
- Help me to trust in you, O Lord, so that you will keep me in perfect peace.
- Help me to think positive thoughts, things that are true, honest, pure, and of good report.

96. When You Mess Up and Seek Forgiveness

Psalm 38:1-3, Psalm 51:1-4

- Have mercy on me, O Lord. Forgive me for my sins and mistakes.
- I repent and confess my sins before You, please forgive me.
- Cleanse my heart, O Lord, and renew my spirit before you. Restore unto me the joy of my salvation.
- Root out every desire and urge to sin from my mind and purify me.
- Help me, Lord, to seek the way out of temptation so I do not mess up again.
- Deliver me from evil and keep me humble so I will be teachable.
- Teach me, Lord, through your truth. Your word is truth.
- Help me to hide your word in my heart so I do not sin against you.
- Blot out my transgressions, cleanse me by the blood of Jesus. Make my heart to be right with you and my ways pleasing to you, Lord.
- Thank you because you are a merciful God. Thank you because you are my teacher and the lifter of my head.
- Father, please remove the consequences of my sin and heal my heart from the scar of it.

97. When You Are Facing Shame, Ridicule, and Embarrassment

Isaiah 50:7, Psalm 25:2

- Have mercy upon me, O Lord, and deliver me from shame.
- Open my eyes, Lord, so I can see what you see right now.
- Lord, cover my shame with your mercy, deliver me from ridicule. Let everyone expecting my downfall be disappointed.
- I pull down every stronghold of low self-esteem, depression and despair. Help me, Lord, to have the mind of Christ.
- Help me to humble myself, Lord, and learn from any mistakes. Come to my rescue and turn this situation around positively.
- Order my steps in your word, Lord, and let your light shine on my path. Show me what to do to escape from this embarrassing situation.
- Help me, Lord, to trust in you through the process and not to fret or make things worse.
- Grant me understanding of the big picture here so I will not repeat my mistakes.
- I thank you because you will grant me strength through this situation and lift my head high.
- Help me, Lord, to have the last laugh. Make a testimony out of my tests and trials.

98. When You Need Divine Intervention
Zechariah 4:7, Acts 16:25-26

- Dear Lord, I cannot do this alone, please teach me what to do now. Show up for me in a big way and beyond my comprehension.
- Lord, please make haste to help me, come through for me in an unusual way. Stretch forth your hands towards this situation and make a way.
- Please give me the strength to endure and be patient as I wait for divine intervention in my life.
- Grant me wisdom needed to handle this situation, Lord, and deliver me from embarrassment. Let not your name be ridiculed in my life.
- Help me to wait on you, Lord. May I not thwart your plans over my life through impatience.
- Help me, Lord, not to do something stupid or foolish that will bring regret into my life and family.
- Grant me the reassurance that you are with me to guide me in every waking moment of my life.
- Give me peace of mind, Lord. You are my help and salvation. I run to you because your name is a strong tower of safety in times of trouble.
- Thank you, Lord, for there is nothing too hard for you to do. Turn the story around and give me a testimony.
- I praise you for you said you will guide me into all truth.

99. When You Are at a Dead End of Life
Isaiah 43:19, Psalm 126:1-3

- Heavenly Father, deliver me from the dead ends of life. Move me from where I am to where I need to be. Open the heavens over my life for the sunshine of your favor.

- Father, let my way open up and light up my path and give me direction to find my way out.

- Dear Lord, be gracious to me and deliver me from stagnation and lack of progress.

- In the Name of Jesus, deliver me from "near success syndrome." Cause my hands to reach my goals and see my purpose fulfilled.

- Father, send me helpers of destiny to lead me into the palace you have prepared for my life. Raise up for me people on whose shoulders I can climb to see farther.

- I command and displace every barricade and gate of the wicked trying to stop my progress. I dismantle every roadblock mounted against my progress.

- Lord, I cry unto you, have mercy on me and let your Hands prevail in my situation. Bring me out from the prison of life.

- Heavenly Father, open the gates of brass and cut asunder the bars of iron erected to stop me from fulfilling life's mission.

- I worship you, my Heavenly Father, because nothing is impossible with you. I receive your grace as I move forward in my life.

100. When You Need Help, Support, and Favor from People
1 Samuel 11:9, Psalm 20:2

- Thank you, Lord, for your mercy and compassion over my life continuously. They are new every morning, and great is your faithfulness.

- Dear Lord, rub your favor on me. Let your countenance be all over me.

- Let me find your favor in the sight of all men. Let your favor follow me wherever I go in life and open doors for me.

- In your favor is life. I pray that everything that has worked against me hitherto is overtaken by the release of your divine favor.

- Cover me with the spirit of favor in my job, in the sight of my boss, colleagues, clients, and subordinates.

- Because of your favor in my life, grant me effortless victory and sweat-less success. Let hardship be removed from my life by divine favor.

- Jesus, shield me with the cloud of favor from the spirit of hatred, dislike, and animosity.

- Put my name in the hearts of people. Cause people I don't know to bless me and help me in life.

- Lord, I pray that you will release a season of favor into my life. Let every aura of disfavor be removed and frustration in every form be destroyed.

- I cover everyone in my family with the favor of God. Let your goodness and mercy follow me all the days of my life.

Steps Towards Salvation
(Refer to Prayer Category #70)

ACKNOWLEDGE YOU ARE A SINNER

Romans 3:10, "As it is written, there is none righteous, no, not one."

Romans 3:23, "For all have sinned, and come short of the glory of God."

Isaiah 64:6, "But we are all as an unclean thing, and all our righteousnesses are as filthy rags; and we all do fade as a leaf; and our iniquities, like the wind, have taken us away."

RECOGNIZE THE CONSEQUENCES OF SIN

Romans 6:23, "For the wages of sin is death; but the gift of God is eternal life through Jesus Christ our Lord."

RECOGNIZE GOD'S LOVE FOR YOU

Romans 5:8, "But God commendeth his love toward us, in that, while we were yet sinners, Christ died for us."

CONFESS YOUR SINS AND BELIEVE YOU ARE FORGIVEN

Romans 10:9-10, "That if thou shalt confess with thy mouth the Lord Jesus, and shalt believe in thine heart that God hath raised him from the dead, thou shalt be saved. For with the heart man believeth unto righteousness; and with the mouth confession is made unto salvation."

BE ASSURED OF YOUR SALVATION

Romans 10:13, "For whosoever shall call upon the name of the Lord shall be saved."

We encourage you to be an active part of a Bible-believing, Holy Spirit-led church family.

ABOUT THE AUTHORS

Dr. Alfred Bisi Tofade is the Senior Pastor of Jubilee Christian Church International-Chapel of Victory in Durham, North Carolina. He is also the Assistant General Overseer and Coordinating Chairman of all North American branches of Jubilee Christian Church International, a vibrant and growing church with a presence in North America, Africa, Europe, and the Caribbean. A gifted teacher and dynamic speaker, Pastor Tofade is the founder and President of Jubilee Acts of Kindness Inc. (JAK), a nonprofit based in Durham, NC.

Dr. Toyin Tofade is an ordained Pastor in Jubilee Christian Church. As a Doctor of Pharmacy, a higher education administrator, and a certified professional Co-active Coach, Toyin is an influential leader. She is a prayer warrior and mentor whose life serves as an inspiration to many individuals. Toyin is also the founder of Global Women Leaders, a nonprofit organization that focuses on inspiring and training women to lead in these end times.

They are blessed with two wonderful boys Christopher and David.

www.ingramcontent.com/pod-product-compliance
Lightning Source LLC
Chambersburg PA
CBHW050600300426
44112CB00013B/2007